MAKING PLAY WORK IN EARLY YEARS SETTINGS

MAKING PLAY WORK IN EARLY YEARS SETTINGS

TALES FROM THE SANDPIT

DAWN RIGBY

WITH DEBRA HASTINGS

CORWIN

A SAGE company
2455 Teller Road
Thousand Oaks, California 91320
(0800)233-9936
www.corwin.com

SAGE Publications Ltd
1 Oliver's Yard
55 City Road
London EC1Y 1SP

SAGE Publications India Pvt Ltd
B 1/I 1 Mohan Cooperative Industrial Area
Mathura Road
New Delhi 110 044

SAGE Publications Asia-Pacific Pte Ltd
3 Church Street
#10-04 Samsung Hub
Singapore 049483

Editor: Amy Thornton
Senior project editor: Chris Marke
Cover design: Wendy Scott
Typeset by: C&M Digitals (P) Ltd, Chennai, India
Printed in the UK

First published in 2022

Library of Congress Control Number 2021947636

British Library Cataloguing in Publication Data

A catalogue record for this book is available from the British Library

ISBN 978-1-5297-6753-7
ISBN 978-1-5297-6752-0 (pbk)

CONTENTS

ABOUT THE AUTHOR

I am Dawn-Louise Rigby, BA (Hons), Mont. Dip, EYTS, PGCE, MA, and over the last two decades I have been immersed in all facets of the Early Years sector. Like all of us working in this area, I am passionate about young children's growth and development. I originally trained as a Montessori teacher, and have Early Years Teacher Status, a Level 3 in Speech and Language development, a Postgraduate Certificate in Education and a Master's Degree from the University of Roehampton.

A key principle of my practice is that all those working with children need a good level of understanding of knowledge and theory, and an outstanding practitioner needs to be able to demonstrate this knowledge by putting it into practice. My concern is that we have taken for granted that practitioners have this basic knowledge.

I believe that young children need a special environment in which to grow and deserve practitioners who are inspiring, dynamic, reflective and passionate about their learning. In a positive environment children thrive and grow, adopting positive attitudes to learning, and the primary way to support this is through inspiring and motivating those who teach them.

I enjoy the process of learning and am excited by the prospect of sharing my knowledge and experience with colleagues and to learn from their perspectives.

About the contributor

I am Debra Hastings, DPP/PTTLS/RGN/DN Cert. I have worked with children for the past 20 years. My previous career was in nursing, initially in hospital, then as a District Nurse.

After the birth of my twins, I started working at their pre-school, initially as a parent helper and committee member and then as a teacher. I completed my DPP in Early Years and eventually ended up as a Supervisor. I love working with children. I love to keep up to date with the research and changes in Early Years practice and am always willing to try new things. I particularly enjoy teaching outside in nature. I am passionate about giving each and every child the best possible start, and this includes being there to support families and carers.

I truly believe that children need teachers who understand child development and are there in the moment for the children, being able to make those great connections and relationships with them and so be able to support their learning. I have seen first hand that children can lead their own learning; they are enthusiastic and engaged when they choose what to learn, and it is up to experienced teachers to support and extend their learning.

ABOUT THIS BOOK

We all want the very best for our youngest children, and we recognise that the stronger the foundation, the better the outcomes are for them. I have worked in Early Years for over 20 years and during that time have observed just how powerful and supportive a play-based curriculum can be. This book focuses on using that to help all our children start their education journey in the best possible way.

I also work in further education, teaching the next generation of Early Years teachers, up to and including degree level, and am immensely fortunate to see so many different levels and experiences, and these add to my knowledge, experience and passion. In this book I am pleased to share the journey that our setting went on to make this a reality, as well as many things I have learnt from my wider experience. I do not profess to think I know and have all the answers, but I am learning all the time and recognise that what we are doing is a process and we will keep on learning, evolving and changing, and I will share with you what worked in our setting and the challenges we faced.

Why now?

The time is now. The concern in the profession is that Early Years is becoming integrated into more formal schooling. It is vital that we keep Early Years unique and that our staff and students understand how children learn best – through play, freely chosen, joyful play. Play is developmentally appropriate and will create a generation of problem solvers, creators, negotiators – fully functioning, resilient human beings, prepared for whatever the future may look like. Our system must be about children, not testing.

There are many Early Years forums and groups on Facebook where the majority of the questions are about the hows of In The Moment Planning (ITMP) and particularly how it looks in practice. This book can help to answer those questions.

Why play based?

Play is the way that children learn, holistically and appropriately to their individual needs and interests. It is central to the way that they develop and the impulse to play is innate. It is fundamental to the health and well-being of our children.

Our setting and our team

Our setting is a community pre-school, affiliated to the Pre-school Learning Alliance. We are owned and managed by the parents of the children who attend and have charitable status. Our pre-school has formed an integral part of our local community for the past 40 years, something we are very proud of. Our team is fully qualified and dedicated to giving our children the best experience.

My hope for this book is that it becomes a key practical resource for Early Years practitioners, that it supports you to reflect on your practice and setting, and that it inspires you to consider your provision and to ensure that play is always at the heart of what you do.

CHAPTER 1

THE TIME FOR PLAY IS NOW

Introduction

Play: it is such an evocative word. It probably conjures up lovely memories from your childhood, maybe long, carefree summer days playing, perhaps in the outdoors. Those long-ago holidays when the summer lasted forever and all we had to worry about was, well nothing – we could just play. Play. When you hear the word, what do you think of? I know I think of freedom and happiness, and I think childhood should be about freedom and happiness; we are a long time grown up.

Play: it is a term very widely used in Early Years, but it is very difficult to define, and we all have slightly differing views on what play actually is. It is probably the least understood aspect of being in Early Years and yet it is one of the most important elements of childhood and is so much a part of childhood. I mentioned happiness, and play is all about happiness – freedom to choose and be creative and imaginative, and to be joyful. The impulse to play is innate in all mammals. You will have seen images of lion cubs, for example, playing. It is how we learn the social rules of our pack. We are born with a natural curiosity, the drive to play, to discover and explore.

In this chapter we will explore the role of play and discuss how it is joyful and unique to each child. We will look at children's rights regarding play and the importance of it. We will discuss how play enables children to explore their feelings in a safe environment. We will consider those pioneers of play who have influenced practice and those who are continuing that ethos today. This chapter will explain why we chose a play-based curriculum in our setting and why we truly believe the time is now for change in the Early Years and that play is the way forward.

The role of play

Play motivates all areas of learning and stimulates our desire for learning – we have so much fun when we are playing that we don't even realise we are learning. Play supports the holistic development of children as it covers all areas of learning.

Play can be spontaneous. We cannot plan for play, and how do we know what the children will want to play with? It is flexible as it can go anywhere and be anything, and is therefore completely unique to each individual child as they will have their own ideas and purpose. Purpose is a keyword in education: what is the purpose of this? what is the intent? My belief is that children are absolutely aware of what their purpose is when they are engaged in play and it is our job to discover what that purpose and intent is and not to dictate it.

One of the characteristics of effective teaching and learning in the non-statutory *Development Matters* (DfE, 2020) relates to playing and exploring, suggesting that this can be developed with a well-organised environment where resources are accessible and available. The non-statutory *Birth to 5 Matters* states that 'Play both indoors and outdoors is also a fundamental commitment to children throughout the EYFS' (DfE, 2021).

As settings, we need to ensure that we are providing opportunities for all different types of play to be explored. This is where an enabling environment is so crucial, providing open-ended resources that are freely available and accessible for all children. In such an environment, children need time to be able to wallow in their play, to immerse themselves in that play and to be in charge of that play. As Tina Bruce (2016) states in her theory of 12 Features of Play: 'children involved in rich play become deeply involved, and are difficult to distract. Children wallow in their play'. This allows for repetition in play, which helps children to shape and build networks in their brains.

The very best way for children to feel safe and secure is through their play. In Greg Bottrill's book *School and the Magic of Children* (2020), he says that play is not a choice; it is critical and, more than that, it is a moral imperative. This cannot be said enough times and is something that should be shouted out loud by all of us in Early Years. He continues:

> *it's not something to sideline because the Adult World decides that it has no value in its systems . . . This cannot be overstated enough. It is not a choice: it is a fundamental right. If we negate play, with all its wonderful potential . . . in its integral power to shape children into the adults of tomorrow, then we are cancelling the future.* (2020, p. 72)

As practitioners, it is so important that we fully embrace play and understand the role it has in our settings. It is not always understood by policy makers, so we need to stand strong, recognise the power that play has and just how fundamental it is to our children's development, not just for the here and now, but for the future.

1.1 Boys with tyres

Children's rights in relation to play

You may not realise that children have the right to play and this is laid out in the United Nations Convention on the Rights of the Child (UNCRC), 2019 (www.unicef.org.uk). Article 31 states that all children have the right to engage in play and recreational activities. Play England's *Charter for Children's Play* (www.playengland.org.uk) sets out some basic principles regarding play and how we in settings can support their right to participate in play. There are eight charter statements, including that children have the right to play and that every child needs time and space to play. These are useful to mention if you find that play is being eroded out of your setting. A well-planned environment both indoors and outdoors will enable and cultivate children's abilities and opportunities to play. Open-ended, authentic and natural resources constantly available to children encourage the development of play. We will discuss this further in Chapter 3. Having open-ended resources allows children to attach different meanings to those objects, which opens up opportunities to develop other skills and associations.

Exploring feelings

Chapter 7 of this book is about how children manage their emotions and how we can support them to explore their feelings. Affording children

1.2 Child and 'marshmallow'

the opportunity to freely choose their play and when they play enables them to act out scenarios. In her 12 Features of Play theory, Tina Bruce (2016) states: 'play is about wallowing in ideas, feelings and relationships, and becoming aware of what we know (metacognition)'. Through role play, children can make sense of their world, which allows them to understand their role and that of others. They can imitate what they have experienced and explore those feelings in a safe environment. It can also allow children to talk about their feelings with others, their peers, but also sensitive adults in the role of play partner. Play can provide children with some control and freedom over their lives and this can be so empowering.

Play influences

The pioneers of play have been a great influence on my pedagogy. I appreciate that theory can be challenging and off-putting, but having a good understanding of the theory and approaches of the pioneers of play can really support our knowledge of the children. One of the best ways I find to think about theory is that it is ideas about how children learn, and we all want to understand that so we can be more effective in our practice. Many of these theories were developed by observing children and being interested in them. The theories came out of trying to understand what they had observed, much the same as we do as practitioners every day. We all come up with our own theories, using our experience and knowledge, so we shouldn't be nervous of these pioneers and their theories; they influence our understanding and develop our practice by putting into words a lot of what, perhaps, we are already thinking.

Friedrich Froebel

One of the pioneers who has really influenced my practice is Friedrich Froebel (1782–1852). Many of his principles have become part of my pedagogy and, as such, I will be referring to him throughout this book. Froebel believed that play is fundamental to children's development and that children should be allowed to be children, expressing themselves through their play. This resonates with me and the concern I have that childhood is being eroded, as there is more and more of an obsession with results. Froebel's belief in the value of the outdoors has influenced my practice, and I have seen the joy that children gain from being outside and finding a connection with nature. There is such freedom outdoors and children can express themselves if they are afforded the opportunity and resources to do so. Froebel advocated for children to do something for themselves rather than be dictated to, allowing them the freedom of choice in that moment. The reason for any play needs to come from the children and not given to them.

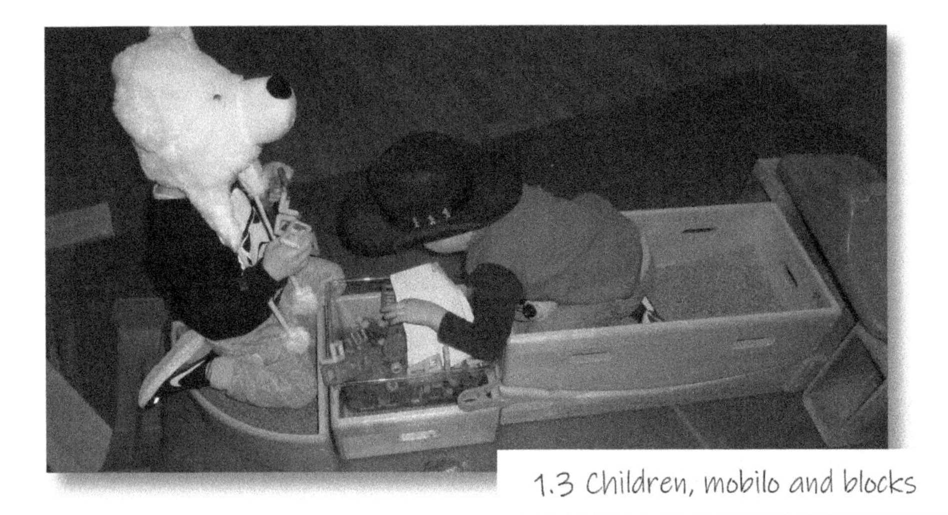

1.3 Children, mobilo and blocks

Greg Bottrill

My students will be rolling their eyes now as I mention Greg Bottrill. Reading his book *Can I Go & Play Now?* (2018) has greatly influenced my practice and

I am always referring to his words and ethos when I am teaching my Level 3 Early Years students. They do get a bit fed up hearing his name, but it is so important that they and all of us working with children know there are people out there who can advise and guide us today, and that those early pioneers of play have continued to influence educators and shape practice. I want those young Early Years students to know that they have the ability to go out and model great practice that supports and nurtures our youngest children; that they truly understand the value of play and a play-based curriculum. My hope is that in a few years we will not have to shout so loud about play, that the next generation of practitioners will not feel the frustration of not being listened to by those who make decisions and that the early years of childhood are valued and celebrated. It is important to remember that the early years are not school. Childhood is fleeting and it should be full of joy, excitement, discovery and exploration. It should not be sitting quietly, regurgitating facts and passing tests.

Why we chose a play-based curriculum

Over my twenty-plus years working with children I have learnt a great deal – the children have been a great teacher to me. I have learnt to listen to them, to understand them and to go from their interests. I freely admit in the past to planning using topics and themes, spending considerable amounts of time thinking of what the children might be interested in and concerned with making sure that every area was covered. I would find that despite my best attempts, the children would either not be all that interested in my topic or theme, or they would not engage with it in the way I expected them to or wanted them to. I would feel that all my planning was irrelevant and who was I planning for? I would have answered 'the children', but if they were not really enjoying the topics and themes, then why was I doing it?

It was a revelation to me to think about going from the child's interests in the moment. It felt as though a weight had been lifted from my shoulders and I realised just how stressful I found planning, and if I felt stressed, how were the children feeling? Expecting children to move from one planned activity to another creates an environment where children are not able to truly wallow in their play. This means that they are not able to deeply engage in their play, as deep engagement equals deep learning. We need to understand that there is really no point in teaching the children something that they cannot do independently afterwards, as that is when the learning happens.

I began to explore my role in play and you may be asking yourself, if we allow play to be child-initiated, what is our role? I will explore this further in Chapter 13 about being a play partner, but really our role is to become attuned into children's play. We can plant ideas and enhance their play, but we should always be mindful of not taking over that play. Engaging in play with children was another key moment for me, as I rediscovered the joy of working with children, which reminded me why I chose this profession. Having the time to actually play with the children rather than coaxing them to come and have a go at an activity of my choice, gave me the chance to have meaningful conversations and chat, rather than testing conversations which can spring from pre-planned, adult-led activities.

The time is now

At the time of writing, during the global COVID pandemic, there is much talk about the future: what will it look like, how will it be and how on earth will our children cope when they will be so far behind? 'Behind who?' is my question. I don't know about you, but I have never been very good at foretelling the future and at the time of writing, I really have no idea how the world will look as we come out of a global lockdown. But I know one thing, that whatever the future is like, we will need kind, compassionate, confident, resilient children who can problem solve and negotiate so they are capable of being fully functioning human beings. As Greg Bottrill explains, we need to make a decision right now about how we treat children, 'valuing them, accepting them, recognising their true role: to lead us out of the past and into new possibilities' (2020, p. 72), and I imagine like me, you want a future full of new possibilities.

I also truly believe in the certainty that children are individuals with their own thoughts, ideas and passions. They know what interests and excites them and, as an Early Years practitioner, it is up to you to discover that. Too often, adults assume they have all the answers and our role is to fill these children with facts and knowledge. We need to think instead about who are these children in our care, what knowledge do they already have (because they have plenty) and what new knowledge would they like to learn? Then, we need to ask, how can I support this? We need to remember that children always have something to tell us; we just need to listen. So yes, I do feel that now is the time for play to stand up and shout 'I am what children need right now, child-chosen play, pure authentic experiences from within the child!'

Now is also the time for In The Moment Planning to take centre stage, giving children the support to have the right to freely chosen play. This will be explored in more detail and depth throughout this book. Anna Ephgrave (2018) tells us that In The Moment Planning is actually nothing new, that parents do it quite naturally all the time, and it is what skilful practitioners have always done – responding to unique children in a way that is unique to them, reacting to their unique interests in that moment. Planning in the moment comes naturally to us, as we do know our children; it is something we do, but now we are starting to understand the why. Our natural instinct has a name and an approach and this should empower us and give us the confidence to join in with the battle cry: play *is* the way!

I am always inspired by people talking about play. It is always an opportunity to learn something new. Recently I was watching a video on Early Years TV – Kathy Brodie was speaking to Nathan Wallis and it was an inspiring watch. One thing that really stood out to me was that he explained that every time we interrupt the play of a child under 7, we are increasing their chances of having anxiety and depression as teenagers. Now I advocate for play, but that astounded me. That is so important; it needs shouting out loud, especially now as we start to think about what our world will look like as we ease out of a global pandemic. Wallis continued by saying that more free play equals less anxiety. As practitioners, we can ensure that we keep transitions throughout our sessions to a minimum and only if they are essential. This may cause issues in your setting, which is why listening to people like Nathan Wallis can give us the information we need to support our fight for the role of play. As much as you possibly can, you need to ensure that children have long uninterrupted time for play.

It is key here to note that Wallis talks about the under-7s and this is where schools can start to learn from the Early Years. In his book *365 Days of Play*, Alistair Bryce-Clegg quotes Kay Redfield Jamison who states: 'Children need the freedom and time to play. Play is not a luxury. Play is a necessity' (2020, p. 24). This really needs to be another one of our mantras – a necessity, it is essential.

In the Early Years we think a lot about the work of Abraham Maslow who said: 'Almost all creativity involves play' (Bryce-Clegg, 2020, p. 5). Whatever the world looks like in the future, we will need creative individuals because we will want change. Rather than focusing on preparing children for a future we cannot foresee, getting them ready for jobs that we have no idea will exist, we need to encourage their creativity so they have the ability to *be* the future. As Piaget said: 'Play is the answer to the question, "how does anything new come about?"' (Bryce-Clegg, 2020, p. 11). Throughout this book, I will give you guidance on ways you can offer opportunities for play in your setting. The environment is going to be critical in this journey of play, how you provide an environment that affords the children those opportunities to engage and wallow in play. The resources you offer, open-ended and stimulating for those children you have in your setting, will be critical for the children to develop in all areas.

So, the time is now and I firmly believe this. We have a chance to make some changes, to allow planning in the moment to take its place so that our very youngest children can learn and progress in a way that is perfect and developmentally appropriate for them, through play. It's time for play to take its place, to raise its head and know it is what our children need.

Learn more

In this chapter we have looked at the role of play and that children have a right to play. We have also explored how play enables children to explore their emotions and those pioneers who have influenced my passion for play. We discussed why a play-based curriculum is so important for children's development. For further information, I recommend reading *Bringing the Froebel Approach to your Early Years Practice* by Helen Tovey. I also recommend Nathan Wallis's website which you can find at www.nathanwallis.com.

References

Bottrill, G. (2018) *Can I Go & Play Now?* London: Sage.

Bottrill, G. (2020) *School and the Magic of Children*. London: Sage.

Bruce, T. (2016) *Learning Through Play*. Available at: www.geteduca.com/blog/learning-through-play-tina-bruce/ (accessed 6 July 2021).

Bryce-Clegg, A. (2020) *365 Days of Play*. London: Sage.

Department for Education (DfE) (2020) *Development Matters: Non-statutory Curriculum Guidance for the Early Years Foundation Stage*. London: DfE. Crown copyright.

Department for Education (DfE) (2021) *Birth to 5 Matters: Non-statutory Guidance for the Early Years Foundation Stage*. London: DfE. Crown copyright.

Ephgrave, A. (2018) *Planning in the Moment with Young Children*. Abingdon: Routledge.

Tovey, H. (2013) *Bringing the Froebel Approach to your Early Years Practice*. Abingdon: Routledge.

CHAPTER 2

OUR JOURNEY

Introduction

This chapter will discuss how in our setting we started our journey into In The Moment Planning (ITMP). It will consider why we wanted to make changes and why we chose In The Moment Planning as the way forward. It will also discuss how we put this into practice and some of the difficulties we experienced.

Why we decided to change our approach

Running a setting comes with many challenges to face. How do we make sure that our setting is a success and what does success actually look like?

To me, success boils down to two main things: happy staff and happy children who are achieving the very best they can. This is obviously a simplistic view. There are many other things that come into play here: not least Ofsted, parental expectations and funding rates, to name but a few. In 2018, our cohort had many children with additional needs and several with English as an Additional Language (EAL). We were all working extremely hard each and every day with less and less time to just 'be' with the children, be that for a cuddle, a story or just someone to sit and chat with. The number of children working below the expected level in Personal, Social and Emotional development areas was high. Perhaps they weren't getting the level of emotional support they needed at home, for whatever reason.

Ofsted rightly places a lot of importance on staff well-being. When staff were spoken to at their one-to-one's appraisals and on a daily basis, they were struggling with too much paperwork, a topic we will discuss further in Chapter 8, and not spending the time they needed with their key children.

We are lucky that our staff have been at our setting for a long time. However, this can also be difficult as staff can become set in their ways and reluctant to embrace change.

How can we improve this situation for staff and children?

Reading research around Early Years and gaining as much information as possible by reading blogs, joining online forums, etc. is a really useful way to keep up to date and current. During some of this research, I came across In The Moment Planning written about by Anna Ephgrave (2018). In a nutshell, this involves seeing a spark of interest in a child, teaching the child something in that moment relating to the interest shown, then seeing what the outcome is for that child – what did they learn? This is your planning cycle done in a few sentences, allowing time for the adult to just 'be' with the child.

Putting ITMP into practice

We will now look at our journey into In The Moment Planning and how our setting put it into practice, including the initial stages, key milestones in our journey and some of the challenges we faced along the way.

How did I go about introducing it to the setting?

We ordered *Planning In The Moment With Young Children* (Ephgrave, 2018), read it and gathered as much information as possible. We looked for training nearby and booked on to it. Meanwhile, we started discussing ITMP and how I thought it would be beneficial for staff and children alike. We discussed it at staff meetings, including the research and training. All staff then attended training for spotting teachable moments. They realised it was not so different from how we used to work many years ago before we were told to write lots of plans and was in fact similar to how we teach our own children, responding to them in that moment.

Difficulties

Like any new ideas it can be challenging to implement change with ease, there are usually a few difficulties. Some staff may not be as open to change

2.1 Children on A frame

as others and it is important to get them all onside. We decided to implement a trial in June 2018.

The trial: June 2018

The trial went well, with adults learning how to write up teachable moments and how to be with the children again. Staff had lots of questions, many of which we could not yet answer. Staff were asked to research ITMP during the holidays so we could implement it properly in September 2018, which we did. We worked out our focus children, sent out focus sheets to parents and recorded teachable moments for each focus child along with group teaching.

Continuing the journey

Following the trial, we realised that our environment, although good, still had far too many resources. We had a huge clear-out, getting rid of lots of plastic resources, garages, castles, farms, etc. Anything they could build with blocks we didn't keep. We also got rid of lots of puzzles, games and plastic toys that were not open-ended. We didn't have many open shelves, so we used our existing drawers but just had less in them. We are a pack-away setting, so our environment can be challenging.

October 2018

In October 2018 we reviewed the way we recorded group and individual teachable moments. Staff were reminded to take photos if possible, to build the child's learning journey and record group teaching activities. It was reiterated that all staff needed to be teaching and recording in the moment for the focus children, not just their key person. Staff reported that they felt that children were enjoying the new way of working and staff were too; they felt more involved with the children as there was less writing and more interaction. We discussed adding a woodwork bench and tools in the near future, with plans to add sewing and a weekly cooking activity. We also talked about Christmas and how it would work with planning in the moment. Some staff were keen to continue with a Christmas Nativity. We discussed who we were doing it for and who benefited. After some discussion, we decided to invite parents in with their child to do some Christmas crafts together. This would provide us with a great insight into how the parent interacted with their child, would build relationships with the key person and be fun. We would also sing a few Christmas songs at the end of term, the emphasis on both activities being very much on letting children choose if they wanted to take part.

In the new year we continued working with ITMP. We attended training run by Anna Ephgrave and it was very inspirational. It was even better because we had already started working with ITMP and had some experience of using it and had some questions we wanted answered.

March 2019

At the staff meeting in March 2019 we again reviewed our progress and I fed back about the session with Anna. She talked a lot about providing challenges for children and ensuring progression in our routines. For instance, at snack time we should get children to cut up bananas with the skin on so they then need to peel them, and teach them to make toast and spread it with butter and cut it up. She also said that we should not ask them to do things that we know they can do or are too easy. Instead, we should offer them a challenge, although we should not give them something that is so difficult they will fail. Deepest learning occurs when children are struggling to do something. She also said that we should trust that children know what they need and that they will go where they are interested.

High-quality interactions

ITMP involves skilled interactions by skilled staff. Leave your clipboard and post-its for a day and take time to just 'be' with the children, just watch and listen. Try not to speak first – be relaxed, smile and never ask a question you know the answer to. Be fascinated, write for them. While you watch and wait, think about what you can add to their play, what can you teach them in that moment. If you can't add anything, then don't. Record what you taught. Did you 'wonder', 'narrate', 'demonstrate', 'encourage' – these are the words that Ofsted uses to describe teaching.

June 2019

By June 2019, we were working well with ITMP: children were achieving, staff were generally understanding the process, parents were providing the information we asked for and were happy to attend review meetings.

However, it was not all plain sailing. Staff still found it difficult to adjust. Some of the issues we faced were:

- Staff still wanted to write up every interaction.
- Some staff found it difficult to spot those teachable moments.
- Some felt that some children were receiving more interactions than others.
- Staff worried we were not covering things such as road safety, royal baby, etc. in key person groups.
- Staff worried we weren't doing specific activities with the children that we had done previously.
- Some staff were reluctant to get straight out into the garden each day, in all weathers.

We simply don't need to write up every interaction; staff have hundreds of interactions with the children each day. Staff just need to write up a few, making sure that all areas of learning are covered. We know all areas of learning are covered, we are professionals – who do we need to prove this to? Ofsted will not be asking to see your planning; they want to know that you know your children.

The beauty of ITMP is that each child has one focus week a term, under-3s have one week each half term, so everyone has a turn at being a focus child and everyone has their week in the spotlight. The way we worked before, there was always the child who wanted to do everything and the one who didn't. The amount of interactions they received was vastly different. This way it is more equal. Staff need to be alert to children who are wanting lots of adult attention and steer them in a new direction. Your interactions should also be more specific as you will know what the focus children are working towards if their paperwork has been properly completed.

It is difficult to look back at how we used to work, we now work from the child's interests and although staff may find certain things of interest, our 3- and 4-year-olds may not. This doesn't mean that we can't talk about it. A skilled practitioner can always introduce new topics to the children but lead by their interests. If a child is looking out of the window at cars driving past, the adult could 'wonder' how it's best to cross the road, so discussing road safety. Staff need to be imaginative about how they introduce new ideas to children.

We introduced a cooking unit and the children have cookery books available in the home corner and are able to request what they would like to cook. Children are encouraged to be as independent as they can with all activities. They follow a pictorial recipe for playdough with the adult only supplying a little support and the hot water.

October 2019

In October 2019 we again reviewed progress; by this time staff were generally feeling a little more confident at writing them.

However, we still had some issues:

- Staff writing was not always legible – they know who they are!
- Not everyone had understood the spark/teaching/outcome of the ITMP cycle and struggled to write them up.
- Not all staff were confident at just being with the children and teaching in the moment.
- Staff were still not all contributing to each child's focus week.

I put together an example of a child's folder so that staff could see how I wanted it to look. I updated our standardisation form to cover the ITMP to ensure that all folders were of a similar standard (Appendix 1). I also put together a 'how to feedback to parents' (Appendix 2) sheet, so that again we were all doing the same thing.

We also rewrote our pre-school ethos to take into account our new way of planning and working.

November 2019

In November 2019 we ran an information session for new parents. This was an opportunity to let parents have a little more information about how ITMP works and how they can support us at pre-school with the process and with supporting their child at home.

We continued our regular observations of our areas of learning. We have always done this to ensure that our environment continues to meet the children's needs. If your environment is right, everything else will follow.

Parents as partners

For the journey of In The Moment Planning to be a success, you need to have a good working partnership with your parents. For any ethos to be embraced, everyone needs to have a good understanding of the reason you are working in this way. We ran the information session – and continue to do so each September for the new set of parents – to ensure that the parents were given the time to fully understand what In The Moment Planning is, the benefits for their children and how their support is absolutely crucial. The session also gave them the chance to ask questions. In this session, we emphasised the fact that parents are their child's first educator, that they know their children best and that together, we would all be working for the benefit of their child.

Such an information session is a great opportunity to make parents aware of what a focus week is and what that means not just for their child, but for them. You can go through the paperwork with them and explain what you would like from them at the start of a focus week and why you would like that information. You can explain about the meeting the key person and the parent will have after the focus week and what that will involve.

January 2020

Although we were working hard to continue to improve, we continued to have issues, but on the whole it was going well. We had introduced more authentic resources both indoors and out, china cups and plates or mugs, and a real kettle, toaster and hairdryer with the flex cut off. Things still get broken but the children were learning to be more careful with them. We bought a lovely wood-working bench which, after initial training with the tools and understanding of the rules, the children can pretty much use unsupervised. Even our 2-year-olds can bang a tack into balsa wood. Children request regular cooking activities which we do in the moment. We have less resources for the children and these are available but not set out. Children can access what they choose. We can add resources where needed.

Overall, children made good progress and the staff had more time to just 'be' with the children. The setting was mainly calm with the children engaged and focused. Visitors commented on the calmness of the setting and how engaged the children were. We always explain that this is because they are following their own interests, not ours.

We held our first training session about 'In The Moment Planning' for other professionals, which was very successful. Many professionals are looking for another way to work, to allow them to spend more time with their children and less time writing. We have since shown several professionals around our setting so they can see ITMP in practice.

We continued to look for new ways to improve our practice and outcomes for our children. We set up a Messaging Centre as per Greg Bottrill from 'Can I Go and Play Now?' (www.canigoandplaynow.com/blog).

Fast forward to March 2020 and in England we began the first of the lockdowns due to the global Covid-19 pandemic. At the time, we felt that this could have a huge impact on the way we worked with In The Moment Planning. We had to make changes to fit in with the government restrictions but still keep working with In The Moment Planning, but managed to stay open throughout the lockdowns. Yes, we had to have fewer resources and more items that were easily sanitised, but the children just got on with their play and learning. The Messaging Centre worked well and was very popular both indoors and out.

We continued to monitor our cohort and the cohort tracking for January to April 2021 showed that the children were doing really well. In fact, there were fewer children working below their age/stage band in all areas of learning. This was really encouraging, which showed that we were definitely doing something right. We are still working very hard to ensure that our environment is always the best it can be. The best way to do this is to audit your environment regularly and make any changes if necessary.

Beginning your own journey

Our journey is not over. I don't think your journey should ever be over. There are always ways to improve. Today, I feel we have generally happy children and staff, our children are making good progress. We are still working towards success, but are happy with our progress so far. If you would like to implement this way of working in your own setting, here are some of the key things we have learnt along the way which may help you in your own journey.

- Take time to read as much as you can about In The Moment Planning before you start.
- Speak to other professionals who work in this way already and, if possible, visit their setting.
- Really listen to your staff's concerns and work on addressing them together as a team. Remember that change is challenging to many people.
- Start slowly, trial some of the aspects of In The Moment Planning that you feel you need to. This really helped us to understand the process.
- Make the paperwork your own; change it to suit your setting's needs.

- Involve your parents/carers in the journey. Running a Parent Information Session was one of the best things we did. Keep them involved.
- Don't worry that you aren't recording every teachable moment; you would never have enough time in the day to do so. Instead, reassure your team that they are professionals. They will know each individual child really well and would be able to show that to anyone who asked – i.e. Ofsted – without having copious records.
- Embrace the time you and your staff will now have to spend with the children.

Learn more

In this chapter we have looked at how to start your journey into In The Moment Planning and explored why we began the journey and how we have managed this way of working so far. If you would like to learn more, I would recommend the following Facebook groups: 'Planning in the moment – child initiated learning' and 'In the moment planning for EYFS'. Both groups have many members who are willing to discuss their experiences, and offer advice and guidance.

References

Bottrill, G. (2019) 'Can I Go and Play Now?', training session, December. Available at: www.canigoandplaynow.com/blog (accessed 23 September 2021).

Ephgrave, A. (2018) *Planning in the Moment with Young Children: A Practical Guide for Early Years Practitioners and Parents*. Abingdon: Routledge.

CHAPTER 3

OPEN-ENDED PLAY

Introduction

In this chapter we will focus on what exactly we mean by 'loose parts' and how these contribute to open-ended play. We will look at how memories of our own childhood can help us return to the child's world. We explore how you can use sustainable resources, particularly looking at 'junk', 'reels' and our greatest resource, 'the outdoors'. We will also explore loose parts and open-ended play indoors, as well as supporting staff and assessing risk.

What exactly do we mean by 'open-ended play' and 'open-ended resources'? Is it the same as 'loose parts' play? The same as 'natural resources'?

The *Cambridge Dictionary* (2020) definition of open-ended is 'an open-ended activity or situation does not have a planned ending, so it may develop in several ways'. In other words, it is an activity or resource with no fixed outcome.

What type of resources/play are we talking about? Well really anything that has no set outcome, no set way to be played with – anything from water, mud, sand, paint, guttering, wood, twigs, planks, fir cones, reels, materials, shells, stones, rocks, planks, guttering, empty bottles, cardboard boxes, bottle-tops, tyres, junk, odds and ends. Even authentic resources can provide open-ended play. It is up to the adults to allow the child to use the resources as they wish and this is where some adults have real difficulty. It is less about what is available and more about how we allow children to use them. As Laura England (2019) says:

> *When it comes to loose parts it's less about the materials you provide and more about allowing resources to be used in unique ways, giving children the opportunity to discover, create, explore, experiment and invent freely.*

How do you allow children to use loose parts in your setting? Are there loose parts available both indoors and out? Observe your children to see what their interests or schemas are and introduce some loose parts to support them in their play.

Thinking back

Think back to your own childhood. When you think about the 'play' that you enjoyed most, what was that play? What did you play with? It is important that you reflect back to your own childhood to enable you to enter the child's world of play.

For me, I remember playing with tablecloths over the dining-room table, secured usually with pegs, making that secret place to hide, or building a den in the garden using blankets, bits of wood, maybe some old curtains, scraps of material again using pegs, tape or string to secure it all. Making mud pies and perfume, using lots of garden plants, flowers, leaves, acorns, fir cones, tomatoes, sticks and stones – all things readily available outdoors. Open-ended resources or loose parts means that the resources can be anything the child wants them to be; the materials can be covers for dens, capes, dress-up, blankets for dolls. The tape can be used to secure things, to mark out roads, to make symbols with, to write messages on.

When I think of my childhood 'play' I don't really think about toys as such, but more experiences with these types of resources. I remember spending hours playing with my Nan's button tin; I remember rolling through her front room on a large round footstool, playing for ages with her coasters – all really lovely memories. We didn't need expensive toys then and children don't need them now. How often have we all remarked that the children prefer the cardboard box to the expensive toy that it came in? That is because invariably the expensive toy can only be used in a limited number of ways; the cardboard box, on the other hand, can be anything they choose. Use your memories of your own childhood and play to help you to tune into the children in your setting. Really think about how you played and what you played with. What are your strongest memories of that early play experience?

Always available

All these amazing loose parts should be readily available in a workshop-style set-up, available and accessible to all the children. It is important that 'the resources are available and accessible to the children at all times, but nothing is set out' (Ephgrave, 2018, p. 37). The joy of these resources is that they can be used by any child anywhere in the setting to enhance their learning. In fact, we should encourage them to take them where they want to use them. So many settings I have visited do not allow the child to take the playdough to the home corner or the small world to the playdough. This is not how the child has chosen to play with it, and if we restrict the movement of resources around the setting, we are in fact restricting their creativity, their imagination and diminishing their confidence. However, we do need to have some boundaries, and in our setting indoor resources stay indoors and outdoors resources stay outdoors, so we make sure that there are plenty of similar resources both in and out. Children learn in a holistic way. Their learning happens through their play. The environment needs to offer those open-ended resources and staff need to have the knowledge and skills to enhance the child's learning, adding, as Greg Bottrill said (2019), 'a sprinkling of knowledge over their play'.

Think about your setting. How can you enable the free access to resources daily, both indoors and out? In a 'pack-away' setting ('pack-away' refers to a setting where many or all the resources/furniture, etc. have to be packed away into storage at the end of each day and set up again the next day) this can be a challenge, but will make you look at your resources in a new light and encourage you to get rid of those resources that don't offer the open-ended benefit you need.

Think about a 'less is more' concept. Whatever you have available stays available all day, every day. This links with the pedagogy of Maria Montessori and her belief that children should be able to move freely around settings and be able to choose what is of interest to them at any given time. Boundaries should be set and agreed so the children are aware of what this involves, and in a Montessori setting they are encouraged to put things away in the correct place ready for the next child to use it. The equipment and resources are all placed in a way that children have easy access to them and are given long periods of time to indulge their interests and carry out activities.

Sustainable resources

It is important to think about the sustainability of your resources. We should be teaching children about the fragility of the natural environment, and this is a good place to start. In our setting, we use easily replaced items, such as twigs, fir cones, acorns, chopped-down trees cut into smaller pieces, shells, feathers, etc. There are many ideas that can be applied to your setting – for example, using leaves to explore their properties in all the seasons, using them to paint on, print with, make collages, make pictures using sticky-backed plastic, using them as decorations indoors and out that children have learnt to punch holes and sew around. The ideas are really endless. Are there any opportunities near your setting to gather sustainable resources? Do you have a garden area with such resources readily available? If not, ask your families.

Junk

In the garden, loose parts and open-ended resources really come into their own. Teacher Tom (2019) says: 'The children I have taught have always been engaged in loose parts play, but you'll rarely hear me use the term. I usually call it "junk" or in the case of items that come from nature like leaves or sticks, I might refer to it as debris' – and I tend to agree that it really can look like junk.

It doesn't really matter what we call these resources, as long as they are allowing the child to be creative, to have the opportunity of trial and error and to focus on persisting at a self-chosen task. Not having to meet an adult's goal, using their imagination and all the while building their confidence in their own ability all leads to building their resilience, all of which is improving their mental well-being.

In our setting over the years, we have gathered quite a lot of 'junk'. The children always surprise us with how they use resources, always coming up with new ways. Places you can find these fabulous resources are charity shops, car boot sales, skips (please ask before you take anything), SCRAP stores, fly-tip sites, forests, woods, beaches, and ask friends and parents. When I say beaches, I am really talking about collecting driftwood and a few shells, not taking bags full of them. We need to share this with children so they learn about protecting the environment too.

Wooden reels

Wooden reels are a fantastic resource and they are generally free too, if you know where to get them. I source mine from an electrical distributor. We have several reels of different sizes at our setting, some painted with blackboard paint, some painted with numbers on, one large one with fake grass on top that can be used as a table, but invariably isn't. One is just stained with garden paint to protect it but not decorated in any way, so it can be used for the children to paint on. The reels can be stacked high for jumping off, rolled, used for den building or part of an assault course. There are endless uses for children to explore. We are not too precious about our resources: they get chalked on, drawn on, stood on, but they can be cleaned, repainted or replaced. We have had some for several years and the only maintenance required is a repaint now and again. Yes, they do get a bit tatty and yes, the children may get a splinter, but again this is all a learning opportunity. Your risk–benefit assessment will highlight any possible issues to think about.

Other resources we use are pieces of tree trunk, long pieces for making zones of play, for using to balance on, to use for assault courses and chunks for stepping stones, some with fake grass on for seats; for chalking on, and for many of the same uses as the reels. Again, they can happily be stored outside and replaced as necessary; it is always worth asking parents for branches to use or speak to a friendly tree surgeon.

Most of what we have is readily available for free or very little cost. However, many settings may not have the same desire or need to source these things for free and so many are available to purchase. I am always returning from my dog walks with a pocketful of 'debris'! When I tend the garden at home, I also bring some things in from the garden – green tomatoes, squash, flowers, leaves, sticks from shrubs I have pruned – again, all free.

3.1 Open-ended play

Our greatest resource: the natural world

The natural world is surely our greatest open-ended and free resource: the changing seasons, the huge variety of weather we experience – all fantastic teaching opportunities. We are lucky enough to have nature all around us, no matter where we live; in the country or in the city, there is always a mini-beast, a bird, a leaf or similar object to be seen. It is up to those fantastic Early Years teachers to feed children's natural interest in these things. David Attenborough says: 'No one will protect what they don't care about, and no one will care about what they have never experienced' (Moorhouse, 2019, p. 21).

Children were born to learn, they want to learn, and it is the skilled adult who needs to notice that spark of interest and follow the child's lead. Children are like little sponges soaking up all the knowledge they experience around them. As stated by Miriam Beloglovsky and Lisa Daly (2014):

> *Children of all ages, abilities, skill levels and genders can use loose parts successfully. Because there's no right or wrong way to work with them, all children can achieve competence, build on existing strengths and feel successful and independent.*

We have seen this in our practice. The beauty of loose parts is that each and every child can use them with success.

We can all use the weather to teach in the moment. Big puddles of water in the garden lend themselves to learning about science, sinking, floating, splashing. We have used puddles to add boats to; we have added washing-up liquid and whisks; we allow the children to experience jumping into the puddles, painting each other with water and generally really getting as much as they can out of playing with water.

Growing plants and looking at wildlife in the garden is also a fantastic teaching resource because we are able to teach children about the cycle of life, about the environment and sustainability. Using frogspawn in a tank, caterpillars in a net, worms in a wormery or stick insects are all great ways to talk about life, reproduction and death. None will take up much space either, so again it is great for small settings, childminders or pack-away settings. For example, one morning we found a dead jay in our pre-school garden. Many staff would have scooped it up and disposed of it before the children arrived, missing out on a fantastic teachable moment. I left it for the children to discover. Eventually, one child spotted it and told the other children. There was a lot of interest and excitement in finding it. The children were fascinated by it, asked lots of questions and wanted to see it up close. I donned gloves and showed them. We looked at the wings, the feathers, talked about its beak and eyes, and I answered their questions. We talked about the cycle of life and discussed how it may have died, deciding that it probably flew into the window. The children decided what we should do with it. I gave them some suggestions and they decided we should put it over the fence where we knew a fox visited and we talked about the fact that the fox might eat the bird, giving him a good meal. Death and decay were therefore introduced in a simple way. The key is not to show fear or disgust at things such as this, even if you feel it, as the children will pick up on it and may well then fear it themselves. We have a duty to teach children about nature, the environment and caring for their local community.

Loose parts for indoor play

Indoors, open-ended resources are still available, but it will depend on how the child uses them if it is not obvious what they are. Lego, Duplo and other construction resources can be open-ended as long as the adult isn't telling the child what to do with them or prescribing a set outcome. Curtain rings, lengths of shiny beads, pieces of material, pom-poms are all available.

Big blocks indoors are a fabulous resource; the children never cease to amaze us with the different ways they find to use them. They build with them – anything from cars to planes. They use them as seats. I recall one child directing some wonderful play as the children built a castle; he explained that the castle had become a ruin over the years and the children were knights defending the ruins. It transpired that the child and his family had visited a ruined castle a few weekends before, which was the spark for that play. The children build up the blocks and jump off them, investigating different heights and challenging themselves. They empty the blocks out and use the trolley to push each other around. Various sizes of other blocks are available both indoors and out.

Supporting staff and assessing risk

Earlier, we looked at staff perceptions and staff preconceived ideas about the right and wrong way to use a resource. Staff need to be reassured that children can really use things as they wish. Obviously, you would be doing a quick 'in the moment' risk–benefit assessment to ensure that it is safe to do. You will have risk–benefit assessments already completed, but for those out-of-the-box type activities such as sitting on a chair on top of a large reel, you will need to think on your feet. You may need to 'wonder' with that child about the possible risks and come up with some compromises along the way. In this particular example, the risk of harm was minimal and the child happily sat admiring the different view from his high seat.

During the Coronavirus pandemic, we have reduced our resources even further and tried to use ones that can easily be cleaned. We were worried that we might lose sight of our In The Moment Planning ethos, but this hasn't happened. The children have amazed us with their resilience and their imagination when faced with fewer resources. Not once have they said they were bored. Sometimes children need to have less to play with to allow them to use their imagination to find new ways to play with things. We need scientists and inventors, engineers and pioneers in the future and open-ended resources to help children build the very skills they need.

3.2 Child and boxes

Learn more

In this chapter we have reflected on our own childhoods and looked at making sure we have loose parts always available for the children. We have explored sustainable resources and the greatest resource of all, the natural world. We have looked at loose parts for indoor play and how you can support your staff and assess any risks. If you want to learn more about open-ended resources have a look at:

- The Community Playthings booklet called *I Made A Unicorn*. You can download a free copy from their website: www.communityplaythings.co.uk/learning-library/training-resources/i-made-a-unicorn
- Loose Parts Play Scotland have a toolkit and lots of additional information on loose parts: Loose-Parts-Play-Tookit-Revised.pdf (playscotland.org)

References

Beloglovsky, M. and Daly, L. (2014) *Loose Parts: Inspiring Play in Young Children*. London: Redleaf Press.

Bottrill, G. (2019) 'Can I Go and Play Now?', training session, December.

Cambridge Dictionary (2020) Available at: https://dictionary.cambridge.org/dictionary/english/open-ended

England, L. (2019) *Looking for Learning: Loose Parts*. Lutterworth: Featherstone.

Ephgrave, A. (2018) *Planning In The Moment With Young Children: A Practical Guide for Early Years Practitioners and Teachers*. Abingdon: Routledge.
Moorhouse, P. (2019) *Outdoor Environments*. Booklet two of the Outdoor Learning series. (East Sussex: Community Playthings).
Teacher Tom (2019) 'The Problem with "Loose Parts"'. Available at: http://teachertomsblog.blogspot.com/2019/11/the-problem-with-loose-parts.html (accessed 21 September 2021).

CHAPTER 4

PLANNING IN THE MOMENT

Introduction

This chapter will go into more depth regarding In The Moment Planning (which we looked at in Chapter 2) and open-ended play, and focus on some of the issues that may present themselves during your journey. This chapter will also consider staffing and how to ensure that your staff are on board with the process. It will also look at the paperwork and discuss what is actually statutory.

Questions to consider

In order to effectively plan in the moment, we knew what we wanted to gain from the process. We wanted to be doing less paperwork and to have more time to just be with the children, to be really able to build those connections with each unique individual.

It is useful to think about what you want to gain from changing your practice. Questions you might like to ask yourself are:

- What made me want to change?
- Do I know what I want my destination to look like? How far from my destination am I now?
- What other constraints do I have?

Constraints that you might consider are:

- Staffing levels.
- Pressures from others to work in a certain way such as Senior Leadership Teams/Ofsted.

- Your environment.
- Lack of money to afford the changes you need.
- The unwillingness of staff to change.

Remember that this is a journey and you don't have to do it all at once. Concentrate on one area to start with and prioritise that area. You need to get staff on board first, so this is usually a priority for most settings. This may be staff in your setting or management. Working in large settings or school nurseries/reception classes, you will undoubtedly have different constraints from our setting. You may not be able to do everything you want to do, but perhaps you could start small and put some things into practice. Once staff and management see positive changes making an impact on the children and their workload, they may be more on board with the changes.

Staffing

Staffing can cause you some difficulties. If you are in a small setting, you may have more autonomy over your staffing levels. Our setting is a charity group run by a small committee of parents of the children who attend the setting. We work with relatively high staff–child ratios. We are not about making profit, so any profits can be used on extra staff. We understand that many of you will not be in this position. However, you can think about how you can access additional funding. For example, if you have children who are eligible for Early Years Pupil Premium, perhaps you can utilise some of that funding to have additional staff even for a few hours, as that will make all the difference. However, you don't need high staff–child ratios in order to put In The Moment Planning into practice. It is about how you use your staff. Remember, your staff will be doing less paperwork, so you will feel that you have *more* staff because they will be with the children and not distracted by scribbling observations or typing on an iPad.

An area where I think staff really struggle is when they want to introduce a new fact or interesting event. For example, one of our staff said, 'What about celebrating the new royal baby?' Our answer was that if the interest came from the child, then yes, go with their interest. If not, there is no reason why you can't introduce it to them; after all, you are the teacher, but it is important to ask yourself whether it is something that a 2- to 5-year-old would really be interested in. Perhaps, if their mum or aunty has just had a baby, or if they have seen a photo of the new baby at home, but generally a 2- to 5-year-old is more likely to be interested in cars or dinosaurs or maybe Peppa Pig. If they show that spark of interest, then go with that and explore it with them. If not, find something else that will spark their interest. Watch for their spark of interest and you will see it.

Getting your staff on board with any change can be problematic, especially with long-standing staff who are reluctant to change, having that familiar 'we've always done it like this' mentality. It can be hard to get those staff to see the need for change. Pick your moment. During yearly appraisals and one-to-ones, a common issue raised by staff in our setting was always the amount of paperwork. We heard this and concentrated on working to help them to see how much less paperwork there could be with In The Moment Planning. Carrying out a trial really lets them see what it feels like to use this process, even if you just introduce focus children and concentrate initially on teaching them how to spot and write up 'teachable moments'. This will give them the freedom to be with the children and learn the joy of reconnecting with them. Once we can freely visit settings again, it may be helpful to arrange for staff to visit a setting locally that is already working in this way. We love having visitors, and it is so much better to see it in practice than just to hear about it.

Reading around the subject is very useful, especially Anna Ephgrave's work and Greg Bottrill's book *Can I Go & Play Now?* (2018), as this emphasises how important and valuable play is for children's development and learning. Training is a must too, as this can really support staff to feel confident, so I suggest accessing some training if you can. I have also found it useful to use the many social media sites that offer first-hand experience of child-led play.

There may be management issues, such as the Senior Leadership Team not being on board with your plans to move to child-led learning, or they may be worried about how you can show that the children are making progress when working in this way. Gathering evidence from your research and using other people's experiences can really help your cause. You could also reach out to like-minded people on the many social media platforms that are available. Take some time to build your case. This may or may not work, but unless you try you won't know. Some things you won't be able to change, but make changes where you can and work with the others.

In The Moment Planning in schools

A friend and former colleague now teaches in Reception at a local school and, having talked to her and other teachers in schools, we found that some of the constraints from a school perspective are similar to any other setting.

Staffing can be difficult, as they don't have sufficient staff to manage the setting, especially if staff are needed outside or are needed to hear children read. They are also needed to manage interventions with the children, and if you add on top of that one-to-ones with children with SEND (Special Educational Needs and Disability), the staffing isn't sufficient, so sometimes In The Moment Planning is difficult to put in place.

The environment for schools also offers similar constraints: children need to be able to access the environment independently, resources and layouts may need changing or adding to, leading to additional costs. Another huge issue is that leadership does not always understand about learning through play. Time is another constraint with cost implications, especially when considering insufficient time to train or discuss any changes, along with concerns about how they will communicate their ethos to parents, what it looks like in practice and what their child's daily experience will be in your setting.

Paperwork

Think about the paperwork you currently use. Who are you doing it for? Ofsted? Management? Parents? The child? What does the paperwork tell you? Is it necessary or essential for informing your practice either as a setting or for individual children?

The *Early Years Foundation Stage Profile: 2021 Handbook* states: 'Assessment should not entail prolonged breaks from interaction with children, nor require excessive paperwork.' A lot of what was written about children before we started planning in the moment was excessive, being neither necessary nor relevant. I am thinking here about individual observations that were poorly written and told us nothing worthwhile about the child, such as which colours the child could name. In the majority of cases, this was simply not an age-appropriate concept that we should have been worrying about. This is why it is so important for your staff to have a sound knowledge of child development and that this is shared with parents so their expectations are appropriate.

Another problem could be disproportionate amounts of records in learning journeys. Some staff produced fantastic learning journeys with lots of high-quality observations and photos about their key children and other staff did what was required. Some children lend themselves to a large folder; those chatty, engaged children who are confident to approach staff, talk to them and ask things of them, these children were always going to have lots of information in their folders. However, those quiet, unassuming, well-behaved self-reliant children who do not speak up, do not necessarily engage well with their key person, who rarely ask for anything, are those with less information in their folder. It is so much harder to get them to engage and often they can be forgotten. They wouldn't be the ones rushing to join your beautifully set up adult-initiated activities. This is where child-led learning with focus children really comes into its own. Those more quiet children may get their week in the spotlight, but they may still be shy and less engaged. However, you will have been playing with them, chatting to them, listening to them and building deep connections with them, and their focus week allows you to spend more time with them, finding out what they love and dislike. All the children's folders will now have similar information in them. This may not seem important to many, but to parents with siblings, twins or friends who compare their children's work, it can be distressing to see widely differing folders. We enable standardisation of each folder and the supervisor will check a random folder from each key person each term. This supports all key staff to ensure that they have all the relevant information in each folder.

It is very useful to consider what paperwork is statutory. In the *Early Years Foundation Stage Profile*, the only statutory requirements (those required by law) are the Progress Check at 2 years, the new Reception Baseline Assessment (RBA) and the EYFS Foundation Stage Profile at the end of Reception (from the new EYFS, 2021).

In schools, there may be additional assessments, either school or academy baseline assessments, termly teacher assessment of ages and stages across all areas of learning, and reporting of the percentage of children on track with their Early Learning Goals, as well as phonics assessment of the sounds learned so far.

Ofsted will not ask to see all your children's learning journeys, but will 'track a representative sample of two or more children across the inspection' (*Early Years Inspection Handbook for Ofsted Registered Provision*, updated September 2019). The sample will include either a child on a child protection plan, a child in need or a child receiving Early Years Pupil Premium (EYPP). The handbook is a great resource to have on your bookshelf. Most of the information that Ofsted gathers will be from observing the practitioners with the children, not from what is written about the children but what they *know* about them.

It also states that 'Inspectors must not advocate a particular method of planning, teaching or assessment'. So, if you choose to use In The Moment Planning with child-led play, that is your choice. Currently, there is a drive to ensure that all staff are aware that the government-produced *Development Matters* age bands document that is being promoted in the new EYFS 2021 is itself a non-statutory document and that you should also be considering alternatives such as the *Birth to 5 Matters* document written by a coalition of sector members, by the sector for the sector. It is up to you which guidance you use to decide where your children are developmentally and you should decide which is best for your setting.

Lots of data collection is unnecessary. However, we do track the cohort just by recording who is working above and below their level of development using the progress tracker. This is a really quick way to see what areas of learning your children are struggling with. This enables you to look at the provision and see where you can make any changes to support them. Using reflective practice is best practice and you should be doing this routinely. We have a sheet on our board to record any reflections as we go.

Parents

Parents are the child's first educator. You need their input with child-led learning, so it is important for them to understand why you are changing the way you work and what you need from them. The way we approached this was to let parents know that we were trialling a different approach. We explained via our Newsletter and weekly update what we were doing and shared written information with them. After our successful trial, we held a parent information session about the planning in the moment approach. We highlighted the benefits to the children and the staff. Once parents understood, they were happy for us to progress. We explained what we needed from them and, really importantly, the 'why'. A big part of the change was explaining to parents that from now on we would be working from the child's interests. There would be no topics or themes; we would no longer be churning out adult-led activities and crafts. There would be no adult-led Mother's Day cards, Christmas cards and gifts, and we would no longer be doing an adult-led Nativity play. All our activities would be child-led. This doesn't mean that children won't do any of those things, but instead it will come from them; it will be their interpretation of what it means to them. If we take the example of Christmas cards; of course, the older children know about Christmas and with the endless hype around Christmas they are going to mention it. This is your spark of interest; now you can introduce some Christmas resources – maybe some specific craft resources and the necessary equipment should they want to make a card. They will have seen cards being received at home, so know that this is a traditional activity; if it is not familiar to any of the children, explain it to them.

In our setting, there are many ways that we have found to introduce a new fact or knowledge to the children. For example, you could use a story at story time, a photo from their learning journey, or you could find something you have hidden in the garden to spark their interest. It could come from a mystery message from our Message Centre, hidden in the setting. It is about being imaginative. Recently, the children were interested in fairies: where would the fairies live in our garden? I joined in and together we found hidden messages that the children were convinced had been left for them by the fairies, which led to them creating a garden for the fairies and they wrote messages back to them.

We think that you will all get to know your children far better just by being able to spend that quality time with them without the added pressure of having to write up every interaction as an observation. Leave your post-it notes for a day and just be available to the children. Sit and chat with them, join them at an activity of their choosing and you will be amazed at what they will chat about, especially once you have had time to build those all-important connections with them.

Environment

The new EYFS 2021 says:

> *children learn and develop well in enabling environments with teaching and support from adults, who respond to their individual interests and needs and help them to build their learning over time.*

Getting the environment right, as we have already said, is paramount. In our setting, we changed our environment to mainly workshop style to make 'everything available but nothing set up'. We had drawer units which, although not perfect for this type of environment, had to do. I would definitely say use what you have, maybe repurpose units. We had a small square unit used as a book box which we turned on its end, added castors and used it as shelving. As we discussed in Chapter 3, we had a huge clear-out of resources and got rid of many resources that were not open-ended. This is difficult, but you can't afford to be sentimental. We removed drawers from units to allow more space for children to see what was available. Get your environment right and everything else will follow. We introduced the units and what was in each unit to the children gradually, showing them how they could use some of the resources, but allowing them to use them how they wished. I remember having some lovely magnetic balls and rods available with the magnets and later in the day seeing them being used in the kettle, in the home corner, and why not? Let the children move things around the setting. We do have rules and boundaries, but not rules for the sake of rules. We teach children to 'Choose it, use it, put it away'. With any boundaries they can take time to learn, but repetition and consistency with the staff all saying the same thing will win in the end.

Planning

Another area that people often struggle to understand is the actual planning cycle that you use in the moment. We explain our long-, medium- and short-term planning as follows:

- Long-term plan is the Early Years Foundation Stage.
- Medium-term plan is the seasons.
- Short-term plan is In The Moment Planning.

You are still using the planning cycle of 'observing, assessing and planning' but you are doing it in a different way, in that moment. You observe a child show an interest in something, you assess what they need to learn, you plan what you are going to teach them and then you assess the outcome. What have they learnt from you?

It is just as you would do with a child at home. For instance, if a baby shows an interest in banging a saucepan, you would probably encourage them to make different noises by providing different resources; you would perhaps demonstrate how to use a wooden spoon and you would provide a narrative to their play. They would probably then start using the different resources to make different sounds. You have taught them in that moment.

What we do is nothing different. All the time you are sprinkling the teaching over the top of your child's play and exploration. The younger the child, the more information there is to teach them as there are so many experiences they have not yet had an opportunity to engage in.

Teaching in the moment

Our staff were worried about how to identify a teachable moment. They had many years of experience working with children, but this was a new way of working and was obviously a new way of recording it, and it was scary. When we trialled this way of working, we chose a couple of children and used them as 'focus children'. We had information sent in from parents as part of the cycle, so already had a few ideas about what parents wanted to know about their child's development. Spotting a teachable moment really isn't difficult and once you have done a few, you will feel more confident. How we write them up is very different as you are writing from a different perspective and should be writing it up retrospectively. Make sure you have the 'teaching' words from the *Ofsted Inspection Handbook* (2019) displayed around the setting for staff to refer to. They are:

- communicating;
- modelling language;
- showing;
- explaining;
- demonstrating;
- exploring ideas;
- encouraging;
- questioning;
- recalling;
- providing a narrative for what they are doing;
- facilitating;
- setting challenges.

These are important descriptors of the way we teach; they will help you to decide what you taught and how you taught it. We use them to describe how we have taught a skill and the 'teaching' word is then highlighted in yellow on our recording of teachable moments. Any language used by the child in the observation is highlighted in green. This makes it easy to see what you have taught and the language the child used. This is how we would also record a group teachable moment too. This is exactly the same as for an individual child but for when you teach a group of children.

Examples of teachable moments

If you are struggling to find those teachable moments think about Greg Bottrill's 3Ms:

- Making Conversation
- Mark Making
- Mathematics

If you approach a situation or child with these in mind, you will always be able to think of something to teach the child/children. If you know your children well, you should never have trouble knowing what they need to learn. Remember to observe them before rushing into their play – you may not be needed. You won't be teaching them something they already know. If your child is competent with scissors, you are not going to teach them how to use them, but you may teach them a new skill related to this, such as how to use a different tool, like a stapler instead, or give them a challenge such as 'I wonder if you can cut out a square shape?'

Focus children

Many people are worried about focus children. How many should you use? How do you choose them? What about SEND children?

We choose about 10 per cent of our cohort per week, spreading them evenly across the term, counting how many children are in the cohort and dividing them by the number of weeks in the term, which gives us about four children a week. We also have each child with Special Educational Needs who has Individual Support Plan targets in place as a focus child each week or fortnight. Children under 3 years have a focus week each half term. We choose them from different key people so that one person doesn't have four children to work with during one week. If a child is only in for two sessions during their focus week, or they are off sick, we may extend them to two weeks of focus so we can gather more information about them. You need to have enough knowledge about that child to be able to make a good judgement as to where they are developmentally. Don't forget, though, that you are a professional and you will already have a lot of knowledge that you have stored in your head about that child, when it wasn't their focus week, but you were still interacting with them, so use this as well. If you are still struggling to make a judgement, speak to your colleagues; everyone is observing that child through their focus week and they may have seen different things, different behaviour, so gather that evidence too. Work with your team.

We feel that you really benefit from having focus children; it is good to have the spotlight on every child throughout the term. There are so many opportunities to observe and teach your focus child throughout the week, so use your care routines: nappy changing, toileting, snack time, lunch time. Routines are basically an interruption to their play. Ask yourself, 'What can I teach them in this routine that I have interrupted them for?' I am sure you will sing nursery rhymes to babies at nappy changing; you will talk to them, so use these as 'teachable moments'.

Progression

It is important to think about your routines and make sure you are allowing the children to make progression within those routines. At snack time, for instance, we ask for a volunteer to help cut up the fruit and vegetables. We start with simple things like cutting a banana with a child-safe knife. We then progress to harder and smaller fruits. We get them to cut the banana with the skin on to allow children to learn how to peel. We progress to making toast; children can put the bread into the toaster, learning about safety, butter the toast and then cut it up. The children will progress to washing up their own crockery and help to wipe the tables before and after use. Again, a whole variety of skills learnt from a routine.

We focus very much on helping all our children to be independent, encouraging them to help each other. You will see children helping each other to put on an apron, put on their welly boots or shoes, fetch them a tissue, demonstrate a skill such as drilling a hole into a piece of wood. How much better to learn from a peer rather than an adult?

We also plan for progression in other areas. In the woodworking area we enable a progression of skills. In the creative area we introduce a variety of skills as individual children show they are ready for them, skills such as joining paper and card together by using Sellotape/masking tape/cardboard/hole punches with split pins/hole-punching and elastic or wool, using different paint techniques/sewing/threading with straws and pasta. Eventually, our children master these skills and use them completely independently.

We encourage children to get themselves changed for going in the garden as much as possible, as they learn a progression of skills; starting with hand-over-hand demonstration of putting on shoes/welly boots, putting on their waterproofs and taking them off, learning to hang up their coats and putting boots on the rack, learning to tighten the Velcro on their shoes and eventually becoming completely independent in their self-care.

Among the things that staff worry about before implementing In The Moment Planning is what should they do about phonics and maths, and when should they teach it? As a pre-school, we have always taught these subjects through play, but we appreciate that in Reception there may be more pressure on teaching these skills in a more prescriptive way. Again, if you have to do this alongside your planning in the moment, then so be it. If not, you can fully embrace teaching these skills in the moment through play.

There are so many times during a day that you can add a sprinkling of maths and phonics knowledge over your children's play. Just think again about your routines: at snack time, for example, there is a lot of maths language you can introduce when cutting up fruit and pouring drinks. It is the same with phonics: teach phonics through play, through routines, at story and song time. We use *Letters and Sounds Phase One* and introduce many of the games and fun activities through play, going on listening walks and learning about rhyming words. To the children it is fun and they are playing. The Message Centre provides all kinds of opportunities to enhance their learning. If your children are struggling with counting, then three dots on a mystery message hidden for them to find is a great way to instigate some maths learning.

Learn more

In this chapter we have looked at how to introduce In The Moment Planning into your setting, including getting staff and parents involved. We have explored the practicalities of this approach to planning and considered children's progression. For further information, I recommend reading Anna Ephgrave's books. There are also a couple of fantastic groups on Facebook – 'Planning in the moment – child initiated learning' and 'In the moment planning for EYFS' – these groups have lots of members all giving fantastic and useful advice and guidance. It is a good place to be able to talk to others about planning in the moment.

References

Bottrill, G. (2019) 'Can I Go and Play Now?', training session, December.

Department for Education (2020) *Assessment Framework: Reception Baseline Assessment*. Available at: https://assets.publishing.service.gov.uk/government/uploads/system/uploads/attachment_data/file/868099/2020_Assessment_Framework_Reception_Baseline_Assessment.pdf (accessed 23 September 2021).

Department for Education (2021) *Development Matters in the Early Years Foundation Stage*. London: DfE. Available at: GOV.UK (accessed 19 September 2021).

Department for Education (2021) *Early Years Foundation Stage Profile: 2021 Handbook*. Available at: https://assets.publishing.service.gov.uk/government/uploads/system/uploads/attachment_data/file/942421/EYFSP_Handbook_2021.pdf (accessed: 23 September 2021).

Department for Education (2021) *Statutory Framework for the Early Years Foundation Stage*. Available at: https://assets.publishing.service.gov.uk/government/uploads/system/uploads/attachment_data/file/974907/EYFS_framework_-_March_2021.pdf (accessed 23 September 2021).

Department for Education and Skills (2007) *Letters and Sounds: Principles and Practice of High Quality Phonics*. London: DfES. Crown copyright.

Early Education (2021) *Birth to 5 Matters: Non-statutory Guidance for the Early Years Foundation Stage*. St Albans: Early Education. Available at: www.birthto5matters.org.uk (accessed 19 September 2021).

Ephgrave, A. (2018) *Planning in the Moment with Young Children*. Abingdon: Routledge.

Ofsted (2021) *Early Years Inspection Handbook for Ofsted Registered Provision*. Available at: www.gov.uk/government/publications/early-years-inspection-handbook-eif/early-years-inspection-handbook-for-ofsted-registered-provision (accessed 23 September 2021).

CHAPTER 5

RISKY PLAY

Introduction

Risky play is definitely something we discuss at great length in Early Years settings. Some of us relish and enjoy watching the children engage in such play, while others can find it very stressful and worrying.

This chapter will look at what risky play is and consider the different environments that you could have to enable risky play in your setting. It will also discuss how risky play can support children's well-being and develop their resilience. Finally, it will share with you how we have embraced woodworking in our setting and the many benefits of this type of risky play.

What is risky play?

Children know best when it comes to what they enjoy playing with, and in our setting the children just love investigating risky play. In our risk-averse society, any type of risk or challenge can be seen as something to avoid, something not to offer the children. Children think differently. Risk aversion comes from the fear that risks are something negative and so must be avoided. Children think differently. Risky play can be defined as play that provides opportunities for challenge, testing limits, exploring boundaries, and learning about risk and how to manage that risk.

Risk itself is an unknown outcome and could be negative or positive. We probably take risks every day of our lives, but we assess the potential benefits or the possible negative outcomes before we take any action. We are conducting our own internal risk assessment and this is a crucial skill to develop in order to succeed at life. Children need to develop such skills. It is perfectly understandable that some staff members will be worried about children hurting themselves, and so unfortunately what happens is that they tend to over-protect them. Many adults who are afraid of children being hurt simply remove equipment or objects rather than teach the children to use them safely. This can actually create more risk. One way in which we introduce children to look for hazards outdoors is by a photo checklist of hazards that may be in our garden. They learn to check for the hazards before we use the garden each day. They are just photos of things like animal poo, broken glass, stinging nettles, toadstools and a locked gate. This is another great tool for teaching children to be responsible for their own safety.

Over the last few years, each cohort has really enjoyed discovering different ways of using the A frame that we have outside, whether that is climbing across or hanging upside down. They are learning about all the ways their bodies move and what they can and cannot do. We have found the A frame to be such a valuable piece of equipment for our children and they certainly love it.

5.1 Child on A frame

Different environments

Opportunities to play in and experience different environments are important. There are many ways that settings can offer this. Outdoors we ensure that there are different surfaces and textures for the children to explore. In our setting we have grass, but it can get very muddy and we found that at certain points during the year the weather made it unusable, so we bit the bullet and put down some artificial grass. It is not everyone's favourite, but we find it works extremely well and is now accessible all year round. We have a hard surface area as we feel that children need to experience surfaces they will come across out of setting, so they can learn how to play safely on such a surface – if they fall, it will hurt. We also have a paved area, which is ideal for a variety of activities. These different types of environments allow children to experience a challenge. If a child does not attempt a new experience or challenge, they will not be ready to move on to their next stage of development, whatever that may be. For development to occur, the child needs a stimulating environment as well as adult support. Making sure that children's play opportunities are challenging prevents children from becoming bored and stimulates their development. Alistair Bryce-Clegg (2015) has influenced my thinking here, as he talks about 'the thrill factor'. He says that children, if they are not suitably challenged, will want to ramp up the thrill factor and this means danger. He has encouraged me to consider what he calls 'thrill, will, skill audit' where you look to see where the areas of thrill are and to ensure that there is a high level of skill development happening to ensure they do not look for that thrill in unsafe, risky play activities.

For example, a few years ago, I was working with a group of children where one of them was desperate to have a try on a scooter. She was very small for her age but was determined to have a go. We encouraged her to try one of the smaller scooters for safety reasons and she would get herself on. Then we just gently guided her, holding on to her hands a little so she felt she was doing as much of it as she could herself. She loved it. After a few months, she was able to do it on her own. Imagine if we had stopped her straight away, said no, it was too dangerous. How would she have felt? Would she have kept trying? Given up?

Helen Bilton (2005) writes brilliantly about outdoor play and areas. She says: 'without challenges and risks, children will find play areas uninteresting or use them in inappropriate ways, which become dangerous'. We found her words very inspiring in our setting, as we worked on improving our outdoor area a few years ago and considered what we could provide to give those risks and challenges. Children without any challenge can often show unwanted behaviour and also fail to develop some important physical and cognitive skills, such as balance, awareness of height and judgement of speed. It is important to state here that although we understand that risk and challenge are beneficial for children's well-being, we are not suggesting that we should become complacent about safety, but rather that we fully understand the difference between a risk and a hazard, and provide opportunities for safe, well-managed risk taking. As I am sure you are aware, a hazard is something that can cause serious harm, so removing hazards in our settings is essential for us to keep children safe and we take this duty of care very seriously. This does not mean that there will not be any more accidents and it is perfectly normal for children to graze their skin and bump their heads. Children have an innate understanding of what feels safe to them and will, on the whole, adjust their play to keep themselves safe. However, we need to keep in mind that what may be a challenge for one child, may be a risk too far for another, so we need to be mindful of each child's individual needs.

Planning in the moment lends itself beautifully to this. As we are going from the individual child's interests, we can sensitively engage with them to fully understand their limits and support those children to work towards reaching their potential. Having strong emotional connections with the children will enable them to have the confidence to tell us what feels safe for them and what feels dangerous, and also what support they may need to push themselves a little further to meet their own challenges.

Different levels

It is important to have different levels for the children to experience. As mentioned in Chapter 3 on open-ended play, we have logs that are different heights and widths for the children to use in any way they choose. They are perfect for balancing on and the different heights provide different challenges for the children and affords them the opportunity to assess the risks for themselves. This could be that they move across with confidence or they may need to hold an adult's hand as they learn to coordinate their movements and develop balancing skills through practice, supported through this by the sensitive interaction with the adults. Having a variety of different size cable reels alongside planks of different sizes enables the children to build their own assault courses. They offer the children the ability to set their own challenges, testing out the stability of the planks and learning how to ensure they are safe to use. This can feel challenging for us as adults, but encouraging the children to consider the safety of the resources equips them with valuable life skills.

Play, by its very nature, involves uncertainty, an element of unpredictability, creativity and freedom, with a focus on the process rather than on any end result. That means that the play must be child initiated, as any experiences adults offer are often highly controlled and already risk assessed. Anna Ephgrave's attitude to this has inspired us greatly and she explains that child-initiated play is

> *allowing children to select what to do. They will select what engages them, what interests them and what challenges them, because it is innate in a child to want to learn – to want to be deeply involved.* (2018, p. 140)

In our setting, we have found that an A frame lends itself perfectly to this. It can be adapted to meet each child's interests by providing them with a variety of challenges and opportunities to explore their boundaries. It is one of the most popular pieces of equipment we have and the children use it in so many different ways. The ladder across the top can be lowered or made higher depending on what the children want to do. Those children who are initially nervous of heights can put the ladder low and climb across as many times as it takes for them to feel more comfortable and confident. Those who are ready can raise the ladder and have it at different heights and angles to create more challenges.

Some practitioners can be nervous about allowing children the opportunity to engage in risky play. As Carol Dweck would encourage, it's all about the growth mindset. If your mind is convinced that any type of risk and challenge for children is too dangerous, you can change your mindset: 'You have a choice. Mindsets are just beliefs. They're powerful beliefs, but they're just something in your mind and you can change your mind' (2017). If we are inhibiting children's opportunities to learn about negotiating their own risk in their everyday lives we will create a generation not able to negotiate challenges in the future. The attitude of any practitioners is very important. If you are excited and enthusiastic about what is available in the setting, allowing the children to experience challenges through play, the children will be too. I certainly do not get this right every time, it is a work in progress. I try very hard to use the right language, to be encouraging not restricting, but I can get anxious when children are testing their limitations and I just need to remind myself that I need to trust the children and ensure that this is well-managed risk taking.

For example, last year two of the girls had made themselves wings, drawn patterns on to represent superpowers and decided they would jump off the top of the A frame, putting the ladder across the very top, balancing and then jumping off. I have to be truly honest, my heart was in my mouth, but I trusted those children to tell me what they felt comfortable with. One of the girls was confident to climb to the top and jump off, needing absolutely no support from me. The other was less self-assured and needed lots of reassurance and support from me. She took this process at her own pace, deciding, with each jump, what felt right to her – sometimes she would sit and then propel off the frame, moving on to me to catch her as she jumped. What I loved was that a group of children got some chairs and sat watching her, offering lots of encouragement and support. Every challenge she went for and achieved was celebrated; every time it didn't quite go to plan, they commiserated and encouraged until, after an hour, she jumped, by herself, from the top.

5.2 Child on top of frame

Emotional well-being and resilience

Risky play supports children's emotional well-being, resilience and mental health. A lack of opportunity to play outside may create even more of a dissonance between the children and the wonders of the natural world. Children's dissociation from the natural world is causing great anxiety for all of us working in Early Years settings as there are genuine concerns that this links to mental health and obesity issues in our children. In his book *Can I Go & Play Now?* (2018, p. 107), Greg Bottrill discusses this problem, stating:

> *we're talking unbridled risk taking, collaborative, expensive play, freely chosen explorations, ultimately a deep-rooted and primal connection to the soil, trees, the earth, the sky, to our very selves. We were born to connect to nature, but all too often our children's outdoor educational experience remains limited and neutered.*

Providing an enabling environment in our outdoor areas is crucial for children to connect to and empathise with the natural world and having a positive attitude to risk and challenge can support this.

In many parts of the country there are children who do not play outside their homes and are often taken to nursery or school by car. The tendency to overprotect children has transformed how they experience childhood and many children have no real experience of assessing risk themselves and have limited opportunities to practise keeping themselves safe. The lack of such opportunities impacts their emotional well-being and the development of resilience and this is where our environment can make a difference and encourage the idea of determining risks for themselves.

Of course, risk and challenge is not limited to the outdoors. The indoors also lends itself to plenty of opportunities for children to challenge themselves and engage in risk. This is where we always need to keep the unique child in our minds, encouraging them to have a go, to be more open to more methods, and that the more effort something takes, the more successful they will feel. Hopefully, they will be more likely to keep trying and develop those skills of resilience and determination. Each child will have their own set of challenges.

Snack time is a wonderful teaching opportunity where children learn to take risks. In our setting, the children love to help us prepare snacks and we give them child-friendly knives so they can cut up the fruit and vegetables for everyone. We can discuss what is on offer and chat about how many pieces we need to cut so that everyone can have a piece, so lots of mathematical language can be encouraged. The children have a great sense of achievement by being able to use the knives and learn about safety in a very authentic, purposeful way. Cooking is another great activity for allowing children to take risks. Even something as simple as using a toaster to make toast or using a kettle to help make a cup of tea are all great activities to introduce a challenge with that little bit of risk.

Some settings can be apprehensive about children using and having free access to scissors. We find that as long as we have taught the children how to use scissors safely – for example, not running with scissors – they use them regularly and sensibly, and are able to practise their cutting skills. We also enable the children to have access to the Sellotape machine. This has a rough, serrated edge, so again, can be used as a teachable moment, as we can explain to the children how to cut the tape properly and safely.

Another piece of equipment we have indoors that lends itself beautifully to risk and challenge is our wooden climbing frame. It has a variety of different components to it, so the children can decide how they would like to use it and what is appropriate for them. Again, they are conducting their own internal risk assessment and developing those key judgement skills, which prepares them for their adult lives. They often choose to remove the ladder piece with adult supervision so they can jump down from the top or use the ladder to discover different ways of moving their bodies.

In their play, children enjoy trying to master a new skill, practising it, adding some variety to it and then adding an extra challenge to it. This allows the children to test their own limits and start to discover what their bodies can and cannot do. One of the ways for children to discover how to learn to manage risk and develop skills to keep them safe is through adventurous play. Froebel (1782–1852) was an advocate for allowing children to experience challenges in their play, arguing that those who engage in increasing challenges are often safer than those children who have been protected from them (Tovey, 2013). I have been hugely influenced by Froebel and his attitude to risk and challenge really resonates with me. It's a comfort to know that the early pioneers of play were advocating for such adventurous play, which gives me confidence in my thinking towards it. Froebel says that those children who have not engaged in assessing what is risky or not will probably put themselves in more danger, as they are not aware of any dangers because they have not experienced any.

We need to focus on the benefits of risk taking, not on the possibility of accidents. As adults working with children, we need to have a positive attitude towards risk and challenge in play, which may well be a challenge for us. If we see risky play as something to be relished rather than something to be fearful of, we will be supporting children to develop their self-confidence and encouraging them to give things a go in the knowledge that we are there to make sure they are not being exposed to unnecessary dangers.

5.3 Children climbing on the den

Risk and challenge through woodworking

Woodworking is a challenge for children and could be seen as a risk, too. In our setting, with our journey into planning in the moment, we always wanted to introduce a woodwork bench. We had read about the benefits of woodwork discussed by Peter Moorhouse (2021) and felt it was the next step in our journey.

Our environment has a 'workshop' style with lots of easily accessible resources for the children both indoors and out. Being able to allow each unique child to be as independent as possible is a big part of our ethos. Woodwork is a skill that many perceive as a grown-up skill, so for our young children to have the opportunity to build those skills is a huge boost to their confidence, self-esteem and resilience, especially if their older siblings have never had the chance to learn such skills. How good must that feel for them?

Our children are always very proud of their achievements and keen to take their woodwork home. Children in our setting had already been introduced to the idea of using tools as we have always built any flat-pack resources and always enlist the help of the children in the task. They are always very keen to help and to get their hands on the electric screwdriver. This is a great introduction to woodwork even if your setting doesn't allow for a full-on 'woodwork area'. They are still having some hands-on experience and it will show you how keen they are to take part and may encourage you to fully embrace setting up a woodwork area.

Staff concerns

The main difficulty with the introduction of woodworking were the concerns of staff. They were anxious about very young children having access to tools that have the potential to cause harm to themselves and others. We discussed this as a team at staff meetings and talked through some of the concerns together.

- Would all children be allowed to have a go, even our youngest 2-year-olds, and children with additional needs?
- How would we manage the woodwork area on a daily basis?
- Would it need a member of staff at the bench all the time?
- Could we manage this with our current staff levels?
- Cost implications: after the initial set-up costs, would the running costs be high?
- Worries about what parents would think.
- What about injuries to the children?

We looked at Peter Moorhouse's work on *Woodwork in the Early Years* (2021) which addressed many of these concerns. We also read about benefit versus risk assessments, which allows you to concentrate on the benefits of the activity. I then went away and worked on our own benefit–risk assessment. From what I had learnt, I felt that the benefits hugely outweighed the risks. I took the assessment back to the staff to discuss and comment on.

The benefits of children learning a skill such as woodwork are many. Just think about the Characteristics of Effective Learning in the EYFS (2020):

- playing and exploring – children investigate and experience things, and 'have a go';
- active learning – children concentrate and keep on trying if they encounter difficulties, and enjoy achievements;
- creating and thinking critically – children have and develop their own ideas, make links between ideas, and develop strategies for doing things.

Woodworking lends itself really well to all of these characteristics. It helps to build children's confidence, their persistence, perseverance and self-resilience. Having to problem solve is a huge part of woodworking. Setting their own goals and working to achieve them also builds their confidence. It is lovely to see children helping each other building their social interactions, their turn taking and sharing skills.

Recently, a 4-year-old girl was helping a 3-year-old boy by demonstrating to him how to use the hand drill. She handed it back to him with his wood and the hole she had started for him, and then continued to offer him verbal encouragement and guidance as she got on with her own woodwork. It was so lovely to see, and he would have learnt far better from a peer than from an adult.

We purchased a basic workbench, but if funds are low you could use a wooden table. We bought a few tools to start with, so we didn't waste money on buying tools we didn't need. Initially, we bought a couple of stubby round-head hammers, tacks and some balsa wood. Our bench has a vice but you could just use clamps. It is useful to make some laminated rules for the bench for children to follow. We also laminated the benefit–risk assessment which was left on the bench for staff to refer to and photos of simple items to give the children an idea of the type of things they could make. Remember, many children will never have done anything like this before and may never have seen a parent doing woodwork either.

Begin by teaching individual children how to use the woodwork bench, the rules and how to use the hammer and nails. We started them using balsa wood as it is much softer and easier for the children to be successful with, building their confidence and that all-important 'can do' attitude. Once children had received their initial 'training' they were able to use the hammer on their own, with a member of staff nearby. It is useful to provide a variety of additional resources alongside the wood such as pieces of plastic, milk-bottle tops, old CDs, string, wool, wooden wheels, paints and pens to spark their creativity.

The children really enjoyed woodworking and amazed us with how well they managed the tools, followed the rules and with their perseverance and desire to succeed. As children grow in confidence, it is still important to remind them of the rules. We didn't need an adult right by the bench to supervise them, but you really need someone in the vicinity of the bench to keep an eye on things. As all the children gradually become confident with the use of the tools, the staff have less and less input.

Invariably, children gravitate to the woodwork bench and may need to be reminded of the 'two children only rule'. This is in place so that two children can be more easily supported and allows sufficient space for each child at the bench, which prevents accidents. For those children having to wait for a turn, it is treated as a teachable moment to help them wait for their turn. We will support them to record their name on a waiting list, either on paper, on a dry wipe-board from our outdoor message centre or chalked on the patio.

5.4 Woodworking

Teaching woodworking skills

The children know that they can use any of the resources available on the woodwork bench. Once children have mastered the skill of hammering a nail into wood, we will teach them more skills. We teach them roughly in this order:

- How to use the hammer to hammer in a nail. A tip is to teach children to use a peg to hold the nail in place while hammering. We will offer them thick cardboard or balsa wood initially to allow them necessary success, or we may offer them a sand block, which is filled with foam to practise hammering nails into. This idea came from the children, not ourselves: the children used them because they were available for sanding and found this new use for them. We remove the nails once they have finished so they can be reused.
- How to use a screwdriver.
- How and when to use the vice safely.
- How to make a hole in wood using the hand drill.
- How and why to use sandpaper or a sand block. You could also glue a sheet of sandpaper onto your bench for children to use.
- How to use a Japanese saw. This is a saw that is used with two hands and works by pulling the saw, so it is easier for children to use. Children are expected to wear safety glasses when they are sawing (children are closely supervised when using the saw and it is removed to a safe place after use.)

This is not an extensive list. There may be other incidental skills that they may need to learn along the way, but this is a good start. They may be at the stage of learning to hammer nails in for several weeks or even months before they are confident enough to move onto another skill. It is up to the staff and child to decide when the time is right to move on. Once they can hammer in a nail, we will also teach them how to attach two pieces of wood together, either by nailing the pieces together or by using something like plastic to join them. We use pieces of milk-bottle plastic; it is easy to cut a used bottle into different size pieces and the children can use them for any part of their woodwork project, joining them, using them as sails on a boat or as a label to write on. Remember, it is important for your staff to feel confident in supporting children to use the woodwork bench and tools so you may need to provide some hands-on training for staff too.

Wood is expensive to buy, so use your community, and ask parents and grandparents for any offcuts of wood, preferably soft wood such as pine. You could also ask at your local timber yard or DIY shop, which may be able to provide you with offcuts. Use as many recyclable resources as you can. If you are pruning in the garden at home, you can cut chunks of branches for the children to use.

Our children love to paint their woodwork after they have built it, so make sure paints are readily available. They may just want to draw on them and are encouraged to write an initial or get an adult to write their name on their work.

I recently introduced the woodwork bench to a new child who was just 30 months old. His older brother also attends and he joined him at the woodwork bench, initially just watching. I taught him the rules and off he went. He was a natural, banging the nail into his piece of wood. He held the hammer carefully and I could see him looking at the head of the hammer to check which end to use. He was so pleased when he managed to bang his nail in – it was such a great confidence booster.

All our children have a go at woodwork. Children with additional needs can take part; children with many different needs have taken part with great success. Some children who have difficult behaviour are still able to have a go; they may just need some additional close supervision with the tools. You may need to do an individual benefit–risk assessment for these children, but there is no reason why they can't have a go. We have found that accidents are a rarity. There may be the odd banged finger, but the child will learn by that and there isn't often a repeat. Children are reminded of safety; they know that the tools stay on the bench and are not taken away from the area.

Parents and woodworking

Some parents are very surprised that we offer woodwork to all our children. It is important to allay their fears and anxieties, which is best done by educating them about the benefits and the very minimal risks. If they can see children taking part and being safe and successful, this will really help. We show pictures on our Facebook page so parents can see the woodwork bench in use, and it is important to signpost parents to this at the initial meeting.

In 2012, the Health and Safety Executive published a statement to address some of the issues around children's play and the trend to stop all activities that were perceived as dangerous to children, saying:

> *health and safety laws and regulations are sometimes presented as a reason why certain play and leisure activities undertaken by children and young people should be discouraged. The reasons for this misunderstanding are many and varied.*

The key message of recognising the benefits of play in the Health and Safety Executive's document (2012) is:

> *Play is great for children's well-being and development. When planning and providing play opportunities, the goal is not to eliminate risk, but to weigh up the risks and benefits. No child will learn about risk if they are wrapped in cotton wool.*

It is so important to offer our children appropriate risks so they learn at a young age how to deal with them in a safe environment. If a child gets a splinter from a piece of wood, we deal with it calmly and we ensure that we teach the child to look for pieces of rough wood where they could get a splinter and show them how to use the sandpaper to sand it down, so minimising the risk of it happening again. If children are never allowed to face any risks or challenges, how will they know how to deal with them when they face them in the future?

Learn more

In this chapter we looked at what is risky play and discussed the different environments that can support such play, including using different levels. We explored how risky play can develop emotional well-being and resilience. Finally, we looked at how to introduce woodworking into your setting. For further information about woodworking, I recommend www.petemoorhouse.co.uk. I would also recommend looking at the work of Rusty Keeler regarding risky play or just 'play' as he refers to it, at www.rustykeeler.com. He has also written a number of books you can find on his website.

References

Bilton, H. (2005) *Playing Outside: Activities, Ideas and Inspiration for the Early Years*. Abingdon: Routledge.

Bottrill, G. (2018) *Can I Go & Play Now?* London: Sage.

Bryce-Clegg, A. (2015) *Best Practice in Early Years*. London: Bloomsbury.

Dweck, C. (2017) *Mindset: Changing the Way you Think to Fulfil your Potential*. London: Robinson.

Ephgrave, A. (2018) *Planning in the Moment with Young Children*. Abingdon: Routledge.

Health and Safety Executive (HSE) (2012) *Children's play and leisure: promoting a balanced approach*. London: Stationery Office.

Moorhouse, P. (2021) *Woodwork in the Early Years*. East Sussex: Community Playthings.

Moorhouse, P. (2021) The wonder of woodwork. Available at: www.froebel.org.uk/news/new-pamphlet-the-wonder-of-woodwork (accessed 13 July 2021).

Tovey, H. (2013) *Bringing the Froebel Approach to Your Early Years Setting*. Abingdon: Routledge.

CHAPTER 6

TO INTERVENE OR NOT TO INTERVENE?

Introduction

When to get involved in what children are doing is possibly one of the most contentious issues in our practice. The expectation in some settings may be that you are constantly intervening either by asking lots of questions or perhaps directing children's activities.

This chapter will look at how we think and feel about intervening during play. It will discuss what the role of the adult is if we are not intervening in children's play, and consider the relationship between the child and the adult.

How do we feel about intervening in play?

A few years ago on a beautiful afternoon, some of the children were playing outside in the garden. A small group were playing with Mobilo in the sandpit, four girls were lying under a canopy enjoying the sun and chatting together, and a group of boys were in the mud pit. All were engaged and focused on their endeavours.

A colleague expressed her concern that we should be doing something, somehow get involved with the children and their play. I felt this was a very interesting point. To intervene or not to intervene: this to me was the question. I looked at the play activities and considered; the practitioner felt that not getting involved was something to feel guilty about, that she should be doing something with the children, that she should intervene in their play. I think a lot of practitioners can feel this way, that if they are not constantly intervening in what the children are doing, then they are not doing their job properly.

I observed that all the children were deeply involved in what they were doing. The group in the sandpit were making various constructions, occasionally talking to each other, but mostly fixated on their models. The girls seemed calm and content as they lay in the shade talking to each other, often laughing and enjoying their time together. The boys in the mud pit were discussing the benefits to their play of adding more water to the mud and how they might go about this.

If I was to use the Leuven scales here, I would have concluded that the children were at level 5 – sustained intense activity. The Leuven scales describe this involvement level as continuous and intense activity where the children are fully engaged. They were concentrating, creative and persisting in their activities. I will look at these scales in more detail in Chapter 8, as they are a useful tool to observe whether the children are focused and engaged.

Was our input actually required or wanted? I gave my opinion that the children were all engaged in various activities and it seemed to me that our presence was not at all necessary – quite the opposite, in fact. I felt that any intervention on our part would ruin the flow of all the play, and what could we add? The children were very aware that we were present and interested in them and what they were doing. They were relaxed in their play, feeling safe and secure; any involvement from us would be an interference.

Do we really need to intervene?

When children are playing, it is sometimes tempting to join in, thinking we are enhancing their play experience. This, of course, can be the case, but also adults can spoil play for children. There will, of course, be occasions when the children do want us to join in and fantastic play opportunities will be created, so observing the play, seeing how the children are interacting with each other and deciding if the play is being enhanced, or not, is crucial.

A few months ago, I was observing interaction between the children and practitioners. It was a cold, wet, chilly day and two children were playing with a muddy puddle. One child was four and the other child was two and a half. They started by adding more water to the puddle and the older child (child B) found a stick which became a spoon and the puddle became soil soup. After a few minutes of lovely imaginative play, child B wanted to move the play on to a campfire idea. The younger child left the play and it petered out.

I wondered whether the younger child had any experience of a campfire, what it is and what it looks like. He had just turned 2 years old; had he seen a campfire in his short life? It is at this point in the play that adult intervention would have been helpful and could have extended the play by adding relevant vocabulary and also the experience of what a campfire is. While it is true that sometimes play comes to a natural end and adult involvement can destroy it, in this situation, the possibility is that it could enhance the play, allowing it to be nurtured and extended.

Through their research of adult intervention in play, Waters and Maynard (2010) explain that adults interacting alongside children as they experience activities and the environment can draw their attention to elements that interest them (the campfire) and offer themselves as 'partner (more knowledgeable or otherwise) in the experience' (p. 480) They continue that if practitioners respond to the interests of the child (in this instance, making soil soup and the idea of creating a campfire) in a manner that supports and understands the child, 'there is potential for rich, meaningful interaction to take place' (p. 480).

Joining in with children's play, taking cues from the children in order to understand what they are playing and the purposes of the play, are some of the ways that children can be supported in their play to extend their learning. Children often learn from their peers in play who often make the best teachers. A knowledgeable, skilled and sensitive adult who is interested in them and plays with them in a way that respects their play should not dominate and take it over.

6.1 Dawn with child

The adult role

The adult role is to support and extend learning through skilful open-ended questioning, authentic conversational exchanges and referring children to one another to find solutions to problems. Recently, on a rather wet morning, child H was playing in the very muddy mud pit. Rain had caused a large puddle in the pit and he was playing with a boat. Child A decided that he wanted to jump into this spectacular puddle. 'No!' said child H, 'I'm playing with the boat and you'll get me all wet and muddy!' Child A said: 'But I want to splash.' This continued with no agreement. I explained to the children that child A wanted to jump in the puddle but child H didn't want him to as he was playing and would get wet, so I asked all the children what could be done. Child A said: 'Jump in another puddle!'

Allowing children to make their own choices, to be autonomous in their play and to wait before intervening, observing if that is required or necessary, enables them to build resilience. Building this resilience enables children to keep trying to achieve for the sake of that achievement, not our approval. Observing their play and giving them the time, free from adult involvement, will encourage them to keep trying, to work things through and to learn from those challenges. This will give children confidence and self-belief.

The timing of any interventions with the children is crucial so that they neither intrude upon nor frustrate nor terminate the play. Knowledge and understanding of theory is a fantastic way to expand and develop practice, and here it may be useful to consider the work of Lev Vygotsky and Jerome Bruner. When we are working with children, our role is to enable children to move into new areas of understanding and development. Vygotsky (1978) called this the Zone of Proximal Development – the distance between a child's actual development and their potential. This potential, according to Vygotsky, can only be achieved if the child and the environment are guided by the adult. Play provides a zone where children are able to set their own challenges. Vygotsky believed that learning was a very social activity, and that learning and thinking could be progressed through interaction with supportive and interested others such as parents or teachers. He felt that learning is most effective when adults support children's learning where they are acting as a scaffold. Bruner developed these ideas of scaffolding by suggesting that children start by being dependent on adult support for their learning, but with this support they gain knowledge and skills, and become more independent and less reliant on the adult. This is what we all want for our children – for them to be skilled, confident learners and self-reliant. Planning in the moment enables these skills to develop as children have autonomy in the activities and experiences they choose and we, the adults, sensitively observe if our intervention is required.

By stepping back and waiting to decide if we are required or not, we demonstrate to the children that we value and respect them to make their own decisions. We can be a positive role model to encourage them to value and respect each other.

Undirected play – that is, play without adult supervision or intervention – is particularly important because it allows children to learn how to work together, take turns, share, negotiate, resolve conflicts and advocate for themselves. Child-driven play, freely chosen in the moment, allows children the opportunity to practise their own decision-making skills; they can also move at their own pace and pursue their own passions and interests. Play that is too controlled by adults can cause children to acquiesce to adult rules and interests – our ideas of what constitutes play, which can mean that children lose the sense of play, particularly the development of creativity, leadership and group skills. We can stop children's feeling of the freedom of play by suddenly imposing rules on them, which they then fail to follow.

Understanding play, what is involved in play, is crucial in deciding whether to intervene or not. Mildred Parten (1902–70) categorised two types of play in the late 1920s at the Institute of Child Development in Minnesota:

- **Associative play**: children play with each other, but there is no particular goal or organisation to their play.
- **Cooperative play**: the final and most sophisticated form of play in which children cooperate with others to create play situations, with each child in the group playing an assigned role.

The extent to which you can and should interact with children during their free play will vary depending on the circumstances. Intervening too soon could prevent children from making mistakes and being able to learn from these. In some play situations, the adult should be a presence but not a participant in the play; in other situations, participation can enhance and extend play. Having knowledge of the individual children involved is fundamental so you can gauge the timing of any intervention. The key is not to intrude upon the play, frustrating the children, potentially ending their play. The skill is knowing when and how to become part of the action, which takes practice. You will make mistakes, get involved too soon or not get involved at all, so you will learn from these experiences.

Adult role if not needed in play

As you read this, you may ask yourself: 'Well, if I'm not required at the moment in the children's play, what should I be doing? What is my role in this situation?' You actually have an extremely important role to play here and Anna Ephgrave's (2018) checklist for this is very useful.

Checklist: maintaining and enabling the environment

The first part of the checklist is concerned with maintaining your enabling environment to ensure that all resources are suitable and well stocked, and

6.2 Debra playing football

that you can support the children to use those resources appropriately. This is the perfect opportunity to encourage the children to take care of their environment and tidy up when their play is complete.

Behaviour

The next section is quality interactions, which I will come to presently. After this, Anna discusses that adults can focus on behaviour, so we need to place ourselves in a position where we can see as many areas as possible. In this way we can address any examples of inappropriate behaviour. It is perhaps useful here to consider interventions when children are having disputes and that again, we need to step back for a moment and observe. Can the children actually resolve it themselves? Are we required?

Quality interactions

Quality interactions is a helpful part of this checklist, as it can really guide us to consider how we can offer them. It advises us to position ourselves and move around the setting so we can be near to where the children are playing, making us truly accessible. This is where we allow our children to set the agenda and we follow their lead. Recently, a child gave me the following instruction: 'Pretend that's your dog in the tree and you want me to get it down. I'm the fireman!' Other children nearby decided they wanted to be my dog, asking me to take them for a walk and throw balls for them to chase and catch. This was my cue to support the play but not to take it over. I could sprinkle relevant language over the top of this play, modelling and extending where appropriate.

These are things we all probably do very naturally, without thinking, and they are all very beneficial. We should recognise this and not feel guilty that at times we are tending to the environment and not directly intervening with the children. The point is, we are there and we are ready.

Adult and child relationships

The relationships you are able to develop with the children in the setting will give them the confidence to be autonomous in their play, be confident playing with peers, decide how to play, what will happen, etc., and to follow their own interests. The children on that sunny afternoon in my first example demonstrated that the environment created in that setting enabled them to feel psychologically safe and secure. The environment is always key and we need to make sure that it enables children to fully engage in their play and part of that environment is you.

In some situations, it may be that you will be invited to join in the play by the children. For example, four boys were creating 'holes' in the outside area and trying to avoid them. I hadn't realised that I had walked into one of these 'holes'. 'You've fallen down the hole!', I was told. That was my invitation to participate in the play and I joined in the game pretending to be stuck down the hole and asking the boys for help. A 'ladder' was sent down for my rescue, I climbed up the ladder and the boys helped by dragging me out of the 'hole'. It is an absolute privilege to be invited into the children's play, and a real opportunity to enjoy their company and develop and build on strong emotional connections with them. On other occasions, you may choose to play alongside the children with the hope that you will be drawn into the conversation and play. In this way, you are respecting the child's right to be in control of the play. This is where being an engaging play partner for children is so important – someone they can trust to take their play seriously.

So, before you intervene, consider whether you actually need to enter the play and for what purposes. Will you be adding to that play, offering useful suggestions, developing skills and knowledge, introducing vocabulary and extending that play? If you can answer 'yes', then your participation will be valuable, but it is important to remember that it is not always necessary or required.

Learn more

In this chapter we have looked at how we feel about intervening in play with children and explored whether we really need to intervene and the relationships we can develop with children. If you want to learn more, I recommend the following further reading: *Interacting or Interfering? Improving Interactions in the Early Years* by Julie Fisher.

References

Ephgrave, A. (2018) *Planning in the Moment with Young Children: A Practical Guide for Early Years Practitioners and Parents.* Abingdon: Routledge.

Fisher, J. (2016) *Interacting or Interfering? Improving Interactions in the Early Years.* Maidenhead: Open University Press.

Vygotsky, L.S. (1978) *Mind in Society: The Development of Higher Psychological Processes.* Cambridge, MA: Harvard University Press.

Waters, J. and Maynard, T. (2010) What's so interesting outside? A study of child-initiated interaction with teachers in the natural outdoor environment. *European Early Childhood Education Research Journal,* 18(4): 473–83. DOI: 10.1080/1350293X.2010.525939

CHAPTER 7

FEELINGS, NOTHING MORE THAN FEELINGS

Introduction

Mental health figures released by NHS Digital in 2018 showed that one in nine children between the ages of 5 and 10 had a mental health disorder. The thinking is that these may well have begun to take root earlier. Why is this happening? Why are our youngest children experiencing anxiety and distress at a time in their life when they should be happy and free?

Coping and dealing with powerful emotions is difficult, and for children, this can lead to challenging behaviour. It is often difficult for us to know how to respond appropriately to children who are behaving in a way that is challenging for us. How do we respond sensitively and in a way that validates and explains the way those children are feeling?

This chapter will try to address those questions and discuss how we need to really value a child's emotions and understand them. It will discuss again the importance of making deep emotional connections with children in order to be able to support their self-regulation skills. This chapter will also look at stress and how that can be useful. It will also show how overexposure to stressful situations can be hazardous to children.

Overwhelming emotions

There is some understanding of the fact that emotions can be very overwhelming for young children and they can struggle to cope with those emotions. They don't always have the language to articulate exactly what they are feeling, and they may never have had that feeling before, so don't even understand it or how to control it. As practitioners, we know that we need to give a name to those feelings and emotions in order to help the child to understand that the feeling or emotion is perfectly normal, in the hope that next time they feel that way, they can cope better. When a child is having a 'melt-down', I have often heard practitioners say something along the lines of 'Oh, I can see that you are really angry'. I have used such techniques myself and at the time had been very proud of the fact that I have validated that child's feelings and given them the tools to start to develop self-regulation.

However, I have since learnt that rather than validating how a child is feeling, all I have done was to dismiss those feelings. Reading around this area, I started to question the use of the word 'but'. We tend to acknowledge the feeling, so something like, 'I can see that you are really angry'. Then we add 'but', usually followed by something we want the child to do or we might perhaps tell that child to stop having that emotion. The timing is all wrong or we can't deal with it immediately because there is something, we consider, that is far more important that needs attending to. We make a good start by giving a name to the emotion and feel we have done enough, yet in using 'but' we undo all of that and rather than validate that child's feelings, we have done the complete opposite, showing them that we have placed little value on what they are going through and that our needs are far more important. This rethinking had a profound impact on my practice.

When responding to a child who is experiencing a strong emotion, we need to make sure that we are emotionally available to that child, and have noticed that they need a connection to us in order for them to settle the nervous system and achieve co-regulation (this requires adults to pay close attention to the children so they can provide sensitive modelling to support them with their emotions) to activate the brain. Children need attuned and responsive adults, not adults who say 'But you need to stop that and do this now'. This can be really difficult if you are constantly expecting the children to move from activity to activity or to transition from play to an activity of your choosing. *Birth to 5 Matters* (2021) discusses keeping any routines your setting may have as flexible as possible and I would add keeping routines relevant to your children. *Birth to 5 Matters* suggests that having flexible routines enables children to pursue their own interests, which reduces potential frustrations.

Deep connections

Anna Ephgrave (2018) states that when settings enable children to engage in play without interruptions for focus activities, the adults are available to

7.1 Practitioner with child

the children, interacting with them and able to deal with any potential behaviour issues immediately, teaching the children self-regulation skills they will need to adopt to support their independence at the precise moment they need to have such skills.

This requires practitioners to develop a connection to the children in their care. If a child does not feel connected to you, they will not respond to you. They need to trust you and know that you are on their side, to be emotionally available. In my setting, when emotions have been high, the children have requested 'cuddle club' in order to feel secure and valued, a chance to build an emotional connection to that child. Some settings can feel uncomfortable giving physical care to children, but what message are we giving them if we do not give them a cuddle when they ask for one? It must always be on the child's terms; they decide if they want to be cuddled or comforted, and they always decide when they want to move away from this comfort. In this way, we ensure safeguarding and that we are valuing and respecting the child's wishes.

In the non-statutory *Birth to 5 Matters* (2021), written by the sector for the sector, it discusses emotional health and well-being and links these to positive relationships with staff and how those relationships support well-being 'and the gradual development of self-regulation' (p. 19).

Young children can experience rage when their brains are at an unstable point in their development. This is when the ability to understand the spoken word exceeds the ability to speak and to process emotions through language. This equals a 'limbic storm rage', more commonly known as a toddler tantrum. Attuned adults can safely contain the rage and help the child to self-regulate and recover. A tantrum really feels like such a negative word to use as it makes it sound petty and it is one I dislike, as actually, the children are experiencing something completely overwhelming and need support.

Mine Conkbayir in her wonderful book *Early Childhood and Neuroscience* (2017) explains that when children become overwhelmed by their emotions, those emotions 'hijack the brain, it means that the "thinking" parts of the brain instantly become compromised'. She continues that the result of this is a child cannot respond in a calm and rational way because all their actions are being led by strong, overpowering emotions. It may be at this point that we tell the child to calm down and that there is nothing to be so upset about. However, has this ever worked for you when you have been upset or angry or frustrated? Someone telling you to 'calm down' often has the complete opposite effect. My understanding suggests that we as adults should talk through possible alternative reactions and responses, and model these for the children so they can process and understand their feelings. Communication is key.

The importance of communication for self-regulation

Talking builds brain patterns for language development, cognitive function and social interaction. Words are vital to the child's pre-cognitive patterning. By strengthening the language centres of the brain, this can improve self-regulation as feelings are processed by expressing them in language. It is useful to encourage children to talk about their feelings and give those feelings names, such as 'happy', 'angry', 'worried', and so on. Being able to express those feelings using the relevant descriptive language can support children to manage those feelings, talking rather than reacting.

Deep involvement indicates brain activity and this happens most during high-quality child-initiated play. A lack of this severely limits possibilities for children to explore and communicate their own interests and ideas. It also restricts opportunities for children to engage in the sort of dialogue that can scaffold their understanding and knowledge of the world around them.

The non-statutory *Development Matters* (2020) states that language development is hugely important in enabling children to self-regulate, and that language supports them in guiding their actions and making plans.

Stress and self-calming

Stress is something we are all concerned about, especially as stress levels in our youngest children are on the rise. Some stress in our lives can be useful as it protects us from danger. Interestingly, cortisol, our stress hormone, peaks in the mornings and relaxes in the evenings, so if the children in your setting have a high level of cortisol charging through their bodies and they are being exposed to stressful situations such as changing from play to an adult-directed activity, they will not thrive and they will not learn. Stressful situations are hazardous to healthy brain development, but being supported through stress can be turned into opportunities for children to practise and achieve self-calming techniques. I will discuss some of these later in this chapter.

Moving from one adult-directed activity to another can be stressful for children and does not give them a sense of accomplishment or personal fulfilment. Well-being comes from children being agents in their own learning. As Piaget advised us, children do not learn by being told, they learn by doing. As we have explored in earlier chapters, I am an advocate for In The Moment Planning and have observed it in practice for the past few years. The idea is that the response given to the children is unique to that child, in that moment.

Mine Conkbayir in *Early Childhood and Neuroscience* advises that it is crucial for practitioners to be empathetic, patient and respectful to those young children who are experiencing overwhelming and powerful emotions. If we do not empathise, if we scold the child or demean their feelings, they will become more angry, and it does nothing to tackle the cause of the problem or give them any support with self-calming. This goes back to my point of not using the word 'but'. There are things we can do to encourage the child to achieve emotional competency during stressful and difficult situations. Think about how you are responding to something which, understandably, you are finding challenging, as everything you do is internalised by the children. This is where I feel that it can be useful to practise your own self-calming skills. This will enable you to deal with the situation calmly, respectfully and with empathy. Avoid punishing when a tantrum occurs. Remember, we need to understand what the issue is and then we can teach the children how to manage their responses to situations they find stressful. We need to make a real effort to model patience and self-control so that the children can see it in practice and learn from it.

We do, however, live in the real world and, at times, will lose our patience. This is to be expected and we should not punish ourselves for this. We need to understand it, respect it and deal with it. This may mean that when a child's behaviour has made you reach your limits, you take yourself away from that situation and ask for help from colleagues, allowing them to continue to support that struggling child. Children can learn from us about how we self-regulate our emotions and that this is a perfectly normal thing to do.

As we model our own calming strategies and techniques to the children, they start to make connections between feelings, naming them and therefore making sense of them and then managing them. This can really help them to recognise when their emotions are building and what they can do about that without those emotions taking over and affecting the child's thinking. This enables children to 'regulate their emotions, thoughts and behaviour to enable them to act in positive ways towards a goal' (*Birth to 5 Matters*, 2021, p. 21).

One calming mindfulness method that may be useful for you is the S.T.O.P. method from Mindful.org. (www.mindful.org/stressing-out-stop/).

- **Stop**. Just take a momentary pause, no matter what you're doing.
- **Take a breath**. Feel the sensation of your own breathing, which brings you back to the present moment.
- **Observe**. Acknowledge what is happening, for good or bad, inside you or out. Just note it.
- **Proceed**. Having briefly checked in with the present moment, continue with whatever it was you were doing.

7.2 Mindfulness

The non-statutory *Development Matters* (2021) gives guidance regarding self-calm, stating that the key person plays a crucial role in encouraging children to find ways to calm themselves as they are calmed and comforted by that special adult. Modelling feelings, showing what it means to experience them and that we all have them, can be a helpful strategy for the children.

Strategies to support children

As discussed, our role as practitioners is to support our children to cope with and manage their emotions. Books are a really useful resource to teach children, in a relaxed and safe environment, the names of emotions and understand that we all have strong and overpowering feelings. We have a selection of books that the children really enjoy for this purpose. We use them for specific situations, but also in general too, as part of our story sessions so that the children become familiar with the stories and talking about how we feel.

Using books

Some of the books we use are:

- *Ravi's Roar* (Percival, 2019).
- *On Monday When It Rained* (Kachenmeister, 2001).
- *The Way I Feel* (Cain, 2000).
- *Angry Arthur* (Oram and Kitamura, 2008).
- *Trumpet: The Little Elephant With A Big Temper* (Clarke, 2006).

Breathing techniques

We have also found it useful to teach the children deep breathing techniques which can enable them to reduce any stress they may be experiencing or feelings of anxiousness. The great thing about these breathing exercises is that once taught, the children are able to do them on their own. Such deep breathing can regulate emotions, but also help the children to focus on their learning.

One of the techniques that we have found beneficial is starfish breathing. It is important to teach the children this technique during a time where they are not upset or anxious, so they are able to concentrate on the breathing and actions. It is helpful to then practise this several times, and to talk with the children about when they might think it is a good time to use the technique and in what situations. It is also a good opportunity to discuss what makes them worried, frustrated or anxious, and how starfish breathing can help them with emotional regulation.

- *Step 1*: You and the child or children will put one hand up and make a starfish.
- *Step 2*: Use the child's other hand to track the perimeter of each finger and follow with their eyes.

- *Step 3*: When their finger is going up, they will take a deep breath in.
- *Step 4*: When their finger is going down, they will let out their breath.

This technique is both tactile and visual, so helps the children to learn it more easily as we learn best through our senses.

Mindfulness

During a conference we attended on behaviour, we learnt about mindfulness for children from Allison Morgan (founder of Zensational Kids: https://zensationalkids.com). She discussed weaving breath, movement and mindfulness together in order to enable children to manage their stress and emotions. We found that through our use of In The Moment Planning, we had created a much calmer environment within the setting, which can help to make the children feel more peaceful and relaxed. Going from the now, focusing on what the child is interested in at that given moment, really helps us to be mindful and truly present. Mindfulness is believed to help to relieve anxiety and promote a sense of happiness. Settings can be busy, distracting places and children know if we are not focused on them, so being present in the moment can help us to engage and connect with the children.

I was reading recently about the value of a 'thinking chair', somewhere for the child to sit and think about their behaviour. It was described as a comfortable space, perhaps with cushions and books. I don't understand the point of such a strategy. Young children don't need time to think about their behaviour; they often don't understand it, so what can they possibly be thinking about? The idea of the thinking chair, although maybe nice and comfy, is still punishment. What children need is compassion and support, adult guidance not adult punishment.

None of this is easy and none of this will happen overnight. It is, most definitely, a work in progress. It is important to emphasise that it is always the behaviour that we find challenging and not the child. The behaviour is the child's way of letting you know that something is not right and it is usually the only way they know of expressing that to you – what is the child trying to tell you with this behaviour? Again, this is where making a connection with the children is crucial, knowing them and the issues they are coping with, possibly at home, a new sibling, family separation, a new house, etc. There is always a reason.

Managing these situations is not easy, but we must remember, at all times, that we are the adults, the children need us to do the thinking for them. Greg Bottrill's advice regarding behaviour is simple: engagement is vital not just so that the children are learning but for their behaviour.

7.3 Three children comforting each other

Learn more

In this chapter we have looked at how emotions can be incredibly overwhelming and explored the importance of establishing deep connections with children and strategies we can use to support them to self-regulate and learn self-calming skills. For further information, I recommend reading *How Children Learn: The Characteristics of Effective Early Learning* by Nancy Stewart. Mine Conkbayir's book is also a great read on this topic.

References

Cain, J. (2000) *The Way I Feel*. Chicago: Chicago Review Press.

Clarke, J. (2006) *Trumpet: The Little Elephant with a Big Temper*. London: Simon & Schuster.

Conkbayir, M. (2017) *Early Childhood and Neuroscience*. London: Bloomsbury.

Department for Education (2021) *Development Matters in the Early Years Foundation Stage*. London: DfE. Available at: GOV.UK (accessed 19 September 2021).

Early Education (2021) *Birth to 5 Matters: Non-statutory Guidance for the Early Years Foundation Stage*. St Albans: Early Education. Available at: www.birthto5matters.org.uk (accessed 19 September 2021).

Ephgrave, A. (2018) *Planning in the Moment with Young Children: A Practical Guide for Early Years Practitioners and Parents*. Abingdon: Routledge.

Kachenmeister, C. (2001) *On Monday When it Rained*. Boston, MA: Houghton Mifflin Harcourt.

Oram, H. and Kitamura, S. (2008) *Angry Arthur*. London: Andersen Press.
Percival, T. (2019) *Ravi's Roar*. London: Bloomsbury.
Stewart, N. (2011) *How Children Learn: The Characteristics of Effective Early Learning*. London: British Association for Early Childhood Education.

CHAPTER 8

REDUCING THE PAPERWORK

Introduction

'Paperwork', I hear you groan, and I definitely share your pain! Paperwork has over the years become more and more a part of the Early Years teacher's day. We really need to ask ourselves just how necessary is all the paperwork that we do? And, most importantly, who are we doing it for? The *Early Years Foundation Stage Assessment and Reporting Arrangements* (2021) states that

> *evidence does not have to be formally recorded or documented. The extent to which the practitioner chooses to record information will depend on individual preference. Paperwork should be kept to the minimum that practitioners need to illustrate, support and recall their knowledge of the child's attainment.*

I actually find this empowering, as it tells me that paperwork should be at a minimum and not the all-encompassing burden it has become.

Everyone always worries about providing paperwork for evidence for Ofsted. However, you should not let this stop you from cutting back on your paperwork because the guidance here is clear. The EYFS Early Adopter Framework 2020 states:

> *assessment should not entail prolonged breaks from interaction with children, nor require excessive paperwork. When assessing whether an individual child is at the expected level of development, practitioners should draw on their knowledge of the child and their own expert professional judgement and should not be required to prove this through collection of physical evidence.*

This guidance stresses the importance of getting to know your children really well by spending time with them – which is surely why we all became involved with Early Years in the first place – rather than spending time away from them writing copious observations. This is where planning in the moment really comes into its own and changed everything for us.

This chapter will explain how we used to work in our setting and how we work now. The chapter will discuss how to use the paperwork for the focus children and the ways you can use the parent focus sheet. We will also explore how focus weeks work in practice and how to spot teachable moments, as well as group observations and recording 'wow moments'. We will also look at how we use blank levels and the Leuven scales and discuss how these may be a useful tool in your setting.

How we used to work

Activity planning

In our setting, we spent many years writing copious plans for structured activities for the children. For example, we would look at their current interests to plan what they would do in the next half term, weeks away, and think about how to simplify the activity for the less able children and how to extend it for the more able. We would set up several such activities on a daily basis. We also had a specific exercise time, which children were invited to join and a key group activity which the key person ran with their group.

Observations

We wrote many observations for the children, using a variety of different formats. We thought we were doing the right thing. We followed what Early Years had taught us about planning and observing. Often the activities we had spent so long setting up and planning were quickly either 'messed up' by the children, spread around the room or, even worse, ignored. A clear, in-depth understanding of child development made it clear that our expectations were all wrong.

Having time for quality interactions

All the research shows that children learn best and show deep-level learning when they are fully engaged and focused on an activity of their choosing. This is where less paperwork can really help you to spend that quality time with the child. Enabling them to choose their own activity will increase their level of engagement and hence the development of brain synapses, so that real learning will be far greater. Nancy Stewart explains:

> *When children choose and lead their activities, they are able not only to follow momentary curiosity in novel stimuli which spark their interest, but to follow deeper drives for learning at the edge of their understanding, establishing their own level of challenge – to work in their individual zone of proximal development as described by Vygotsky.* (2011, p. 56)

I have mentioned before that some practitioners can find theory remote and challenging, but it can really support us to make sense of what we observe in our children.

Child-led play is perfect for all children no matter their background, whether they have additional needs and whatever their gender or sexuality, because you are working with each unique child and following their individual interests. You are assessing, planning and evaluating in that child's moment, so responding to their needs in that moment and teaching them in that moment. This means that what you are teaching them will always be developmentally appropriate for each child.

In The Moment Planning is not a new concept. The National Strategies document *Learning, Playing and Interacting: Good Practice in the Early Years Foundation Stage* (first published in 2009) talks about child-initiated activity and adult-led activities. It gives a definition of play and talks about the positive dispositions for learning. It looks at the Observation, Assessment and Planning cycle, and discusses how children 'are experiencing and learning in the here and now, not storing up their questions until tomorrow or next week. It is in that moment of curiosity, puzzlement, effort or interest – the "teachable moment" – that skilful adult makes a difference.' So, for those of you who are concerned about starting your journey into In The Moment Planning, the drive for planning in this way has been around for many years and the evidence is there to support you in your journey. I really believe you will not regret it.

Children should be able to choose their own learning. How do they know what they want to learn? It is up to you as skilled and sensitive practitioners to support this. They may show an interest in a worm in the garden. The skilled teacher will know that the particular child struggles with, for example, fine motor skills, so they will suggest or wonder if the child would like to draw or paint a worm, or even make a home for it – anything that will provide the child with the fine motor skills practice they need. The spark always comes from the child, from their interest. The skilful teacher uses that spark to teach the child a skill or add to their knowledge in that moment, after quickly assessing what the child needs to learn. The adult then identifies what learning occurred for that child in that moment – the outcome.

Focus children and paperwork

We find that what works best for our setting and our children is to focus on 10 per cent of our cohort, which is approximately three children per week.

Our children with special educational needs are focused on each week, as they are always working on targets on their individual support plan. Our under-threes have a focus week each half term, as they are making progress more quickly than the older children.

The process we use for our paperwork is as follows:

- The Parent Focus Sheet is sent out to the parent/carer of the focus children.
- The parent returns the paperwork and photos – currently via email to avoid the transfer of paperwork between home and the setting.
- Learning journey: a focus record sheet is put up on a board with focus points for the child from a key person and parents. If this is an existing child, they will have had focus points from their previous focus week.
- All staff complete records of 'teachable moments'.
- Staff use other tools to record assessments if necessary.
- The key person talks to the child about their photos from home and records their words.
- The key person updates the child's progress tracker to indicate where the child is developmentally.
- The key person writes a summary of the child's learning and development guided by the focus week observations.
- A summary is shared with parents at a face-to-face meeting; currently, this is emailed.

We will now explore some of the paperwork outlined above in more detail.

Parent Focus Sheet

The first step of the process is to send out the Parent Focus Sheet. This sheet asks for information about the child at home, anything special that is happening at home and anything that parents would like to tell us about their child. It is a vital link with home and acknowledges parents as their child's first educator and supports our partnership working with them. It asks for some photos of the child with their family or at play, out and about. It is important to know what is happening at home so we can support the child or praise their achievements outside of the setting. As importantly, it is a way for parents to express any concerns about their child's development. This is a good way to understand the parental expectations too. We have many parents who expect their child to be able to write at 3 or 4 years old and work hard at home to get them to learn the alphabet, when this is not always developmentally appropriate.

Photos from home are another assessment tool for recording children's development. Does the child recognise the people in the photos and the places? Can they tell you about a memory from the photos? We record word-for-word what they say to produce an accurate account. Over their time in the setting, this builds a picture of their speech, understanding, vocabulary, memory, willingness to talk to the adult and confidence in sharing this personal information. Children love seeing themselves and their family in photos, and we find that these photos can be revisited and enjoyed in their learning journey time after time. We store them in an A4 display book, but you can use a scrapbook or similar. They are kept on a unit in the main hall so that children can access them freely and talk about them with staff or their peers. Alternatively, you could use the many online platforms for recording this information.

Some parents fail to return the focus sheet or any photos. It is really important to try to understand why they haven't. Is it that you haven't yet built a good working relationship with the parents, or possibly that they don't have the facility to print out the paperwork, or fill it out, or email it back? You could find out if they would prefer a paper copy, or simply email the answers or, even better, tell you their answers. Some parents may not have a camera, so you could lend them one. For some parents, English may not be their first language and they may not have the language skills to be able to understand the form. Could you provide it in their home language? Talking to the parents and finding out what is making it difficult for them to return the paperwork will probably encourage them to become more engaged with the process.

Another way in which we have increased parental engagement in our planning process is to run information sessions for parents, which we try to run early in the year and enables them to understand what you are trying to achieve and how you work. If they understand your processes, hopefully they will be more engaged and will use the same teaching methods at home. We explain that In The Moment Planning is really what a parent does at home anyway, responding to their child in the moment, and we have found it a very beneficial way to engage with our parents.

Learning Journey: focus record sheet

A Learning Journey focus record sheet is displayed at the start of the child's focus week. If the child has an existing focus, this is recorded. It can be a key person chosen focus or a parent chosen focus or a combination of both. We use the term 'focus' here instead of 'next steps'. 'Next steps' are addressed in the moment when they are spotted. We display the sheet on a large pin-board, but you can use what you have available. We have two Learning Journeys, one for the under-threes and one for the over-threes, but there isn't much difference in the sheets and you could just as easily use a blank A4 sheet of paper. Make it easy for yourselves.

Recording 'teachable moments'

All staff now focus on each focus child, writing short records of the teachable moments they have had with that child. How you record this is up to you. We use post-it notes and stick them on to the Learning Journey record, or you can just write directly on to the A4 sheet. Again, it is whatever works for you in your setting.

What is a teachable moment? It is that moment that you notice a spark of interest in the child. That spark could be anything. As the teacher, you will then see what teaching you can add. If you don't think you can add anything to their play, then perhaps you don't need to. Think back to intervening or not intervening, which was described in Chapter 6. If you are going to teach something, then think about the Ofsted definition of teaching taken from the *Early Years Inspection Handbook* (2021):

> *Teaching should not be taken to imply a 'top down' or formal way of working. It is a broad term that covers the many different ways in which adults help young children learn. It includes their interactions with children during planned and child-initiated play and activities: communicating and modelling language, showing, explaining, demonstrating, exploring ideas, encouraging, questioning, recalling, providing a narrative for what they are doing, facilitating and setting challenges.*

These are the words you will use when you write up your record of the teachable moment. We found that it was useful to display these words for staff, at least until they were confident using them.

How to write up a teachable moment

We will now look at what a teachable moment may look like in practice. (E) is the initial of the child, (A) is the adult. When you record the 'teaching' the adult has provided in your observation, the teaching will be highlighted in yellow and the child's speech will be highlighted in green, which enables them to be seen easily. For the purpose of seeing it here, we have used bold for the child's speech and italics for the teaching.

- (E) noticed a worm in the garden. (This is the spark of interest shown by the child; the adult then assesses what to teach.)
- (A) *demonstrated* how to gently pick up the worm on the spade.
- (E) asked '**What does it eat?**'
- (A) *encouraged* (E) to look in the book about mini-beasts to find out (the teaching).
- (E) found the worm in the book and with the help of (A) learned that worms eat leaves and dead grass. (E) found some leaves for the worm (the outcome).

We make sure that we write up our teachable moments retrospectively. This prevents you from losing sight of the teachable moment when you are in the middle of it with the child. You can write yourself a few quick notes if you think you will forget, especially when recording specifics such as speech. Some settings use electronic recording systems, iPads or similar. We use pen and paper, but again it is up to you and what suits your particular setting. You can also use a camera to record a short video clip of the moment and write it up later. We try to take a photo of part of the teachable moment, or a few photos showing a process and outcome. Photos are printed and added to the gallery on the child's Learning Journey record. Many settings use Tapestry or similar recording systems, and these work just as well as a recording platform.

Group observations

As well as individual observations of teachable moments, we record some 'group teachable moments'. These occur when a group of children are taught something in the moment, although it is still child-initiated learning. A record sheet is used. We record observations on some strips kept in the garden and then stick them on the group record. A photo is also used to record the teachable moment. A new group record sheet is used each week. We have just started storing these in a folder that the children can also access so they are reminded about some of the activities they have initiated together.

'Wow' moments

'Wow' moments are recorded for any child (not just a focus child) who does something that they haven't done independently before. That moment you think 'Wow, that's amazing'. Again, a 'wow' moment can be recorded on a post-it note and they are then added to the child's Learning Journey.

Progress tracker

The progress tracker is completed after looking at the child's focus week observations and using your own professional judgement regarding where you think the child is working. You may have your own progress tracker. Our tracker enables us to record whether the child is emerging, developing or secure in their development in that area of learning. This is based on *Development Matters*, 2017. However, the new *Development Matters* document, September 2020, is very different in as much as the age bands are

Birth to Three, 3–4 years and children in Reception, so there are only three bands as opposed to the current six bands. I feel that the emerging, developing or secure labels will be useful going forward. Remember that the *Development Matters* document is not statutory, so you could use another method to decide on your child's development, such as the new *Birth to 5 Matters* (2021) guidance by the sector, for the sector.

Summary

The summary is written by the child's key person and we like to write them so that they are a positive and personal message about the child's development for the parents or carers. Obviously, sometimes there are negative things to report, but we try and do this in a thoughtful way. We encourage the parent to make comments on the summary (see Appendix 5). The summary is normally shared with the parent in a face-to-face meeting, but currently is shared via email. The key person and parent will decide on an area for the child to focus on until their next focus week. We provide the parents/carer with some ideas to work on at home to meet that focus.

Other assessment tools

Many other assessment tools are available to us. These do not have to be used, and again it is up to you and what you feel works most appropriately for you in your settings.

The new *Development Matters Guidance* (2021) states: 'assessment is about noticing what children can do and what they know. It is not about lots of data and evidence.' It continues: 'before assessing children, it's a good idea to think about whether the assessments will be useful'. This is important or you will end up with a lot of assessments that you really don't need, and of course we are working on reducing the paperwork.

Every Child A Talker (ECAT)

Communication and language, as we all know, is a prime area of learning and so, is a vital area to assess. If the child is having difficulty communicating, it will be difficult for us to assess them in other areas, so it is important to identify any difficulties early on and provide support to the child. We use the Every Child a Talker (ECAT) assessment tool to assess a child's communication skills.

Every Child a Talker is a National Strategies document published in 2008. This national project was set up to try to address concerns about high levels of 'language impoverishment' in the UK. It aimed to develop the communication and language skills of children from birth to 5 years. It looked at how children's language difficulties were also affecting their progress in school and their life chances.

This tool is completed initially when the child first starts with us as part of their baseline assessment and then again during the child's focus week. It is a great tool to share with other professionals when you are concerned about language and communication delay and to complete when gathering evidence to refer to Speech and Language Therapy, Multi-disciplinary Assessment teams and when requesting extra funding for children with additional needs.

The ECAT tool is broken down into four areas: Listening and Attention, Understanding (Receptive Language), Talking (Expressive Language) and Social Communication. It provides statements in age bands. The teacher then highlights which age band they think is the best fit for that child using a mixture of observations and professional judgements. This tool can be used for children with English as an Additional Language too, but you will need to discuss with the parent which band they think their child is working within in their home language. A useful table is attached to the form which provides guidance on typical development of speech sounds. It also has checkpoint statements highlighted in the monitoring tool to help remind you at what age certain skills should be present. A useful user guidance is also available on the tool .

Blank level

Another tool that we use is a Blank level assessment tool (see Appendix 4). We learnt about this tool when we completed the Elklan 'Speech and Language Support for the under 5s' course several years ago. This is a course developed by Speech and Language therapists and was one of the best courses I have attended. We learnt about the Blank Language Scheme or the Language of Learning model, which is a model used to encourage children's verbal reasoning and abstract language. It was devised by Blank, Rose and Berlin in 1978. It looks at the different levels of verbal reasoning, breaking them down into smaller steps. The way in which you decide at what level the child is working is by reading a story with them on a one-to-one basis and asking them questions from each level in order. If they can answer all the Level 2 questions, the child is working at Level 2. You can use any simple children's book you like, but will need to write your own questions in line with the levels above. You can find questions on the internet too, and more details of the Blank level model. You can also buy the Early Language Builders book from Elklan (www.elklan.co.uk).

We currently use this tool for each child during their focus week, but really if you know where the child is working with their understanding, you can use it for those children you have concerns about. It is also great for helping you gauge where to pitch your language and questions to the child. This helps you to work with the child at their level of understanding – for instance, if a child is functioning at level 2, 80 per cent of your questions should be at level 2. You can also ask them some questions from level 3, but not from level 4. Of course, always be sensitive to over-questioning children as some find this stressful – the blank levels can really support staff in understanding this.

Leuven scales

Another extremely useful tool is the Leuven Scales of Well-being and Involvement (2011). See Appendix 3 for more detail. This was written by Ferre Laevers and it helps you to understand how focused and settled the children are in the setting. According to Laevers, if the child shows high levels of both well-being and involvement, this is when deep learning is likely to occur.

If a child shows low-level well-being, they may also be showing more extreme behaviours and so would not be open to learning. If a child's personal, social and emotional development is on track, they should be showing high levels of well-being.

The Leuven scales are used following observation and assessment, primarily of those children you have concerns about. Children, like adults, feel differently on different days and on different weeks, so it is important not to make a quick judgement but to do several observations before you do so. They are really useful when new children are joining the setting and settling in. Once the assessments have been completed, you can reflect on your setting and practice, and make any changes that would help those children to show higher levels of well-being and involvement.

Constant reflection

We review how we feel things are going with In the Moment Planning at our half-termly staff meeting. It is not all plain sailing and there are often things that need some discussion. For example, it may be that staff are not completing sufficient observations for the focus children. Staff should all complete observations of the focus children – in the garden, indoors, at snack time, lunch time, story time and even during toileting or nappy changing.

Some staff may also struggle to keep the child's Learning Journey in a manageable order. Here are a few things that I implemented to help support staff in my setting:

- I put together an example of a child's folder for staff. I updated our standardisation form to cover ITMP so that all folders are of a similar standard.
- It became evident that not all staff were providing the same level of feedback to the parents following the child's focus week, so I put together a 'how to feedback to parents sheet' to support staff.
- It is vital to keep reflecting on your paperwork. Does it still work for you? Sometimes just a different cohort of children can need a slightly different approach. Be confident to change your paperwork as you need to.
- Include copies of relevant paperwork.

Learn more

In this chapter we have looked at how we used to work and discussed that we wanted to have more time for quality interactions with children. We explored the paperwork you could use for the focus children as well as the parent focus sheet. We looked at recording teachable moments, group observations and wow moments. We explored the progress tracker as well as other assessment tools, and discussed the need for constant reflection. One of the main reasons for changes made to the EYFS guidance for September 2021 is to reduce the workload for staff. I am sure that all of you will be keen to learn more about how to reduce the paperwork in your settings.

- As a starting point, you should look at the EYFS Framework: https://assets.publishing.service.gov.uk/government/uploads/system/uploads/attachment_data/file/974907/EYFS_framework_-_March_2021.pdf
- To find out specifically what Ofsted expect to see in regard to written records: https://help-for-early-years-providers.education.gov.uk/
- To learn more about blank levels, look at: https://childspeechbedfordshire.nhs.uk/wp-content/uploads/2020/07/Blank-level-2.pdf

References

Department for Children, Schools and Families (2008) *Every Child a Talker: Guidance for Early Language Lead Practitioners: The National Strategies Early Years*. DCSF. Crown copyright. Available at: www.teachernet.gov.uk/publications (accessed 21 September 2021).

Department for Schools, Children & Families (2009) *National Strategies: Learning, Playing and Interacting. Good Practice in the Early Years Foundation Stage*. DCSF. Crown copyright. Available at: www.teachernet.gov.uk/publications (accessed 21 September 2021).

Department for Education (2021) *Development Matters Guidance: Non-statutory Curriculum Guidance for the Early Years*. DfE. Crown copyright.

Early Years Coalition (2021) *Birth to 5 Matters*. St Albans: Early Education: The British Association for Early Childhood Education. Available at: www.birthto5matters.org.uk (accessed 21 September 2021).

Ofsted (2021) *The Early Years Inspection Handbook for Ofsted-registered Provision*. Ofsted. Crown copyright.

Standards and Testing Agency (2019) *Early Years Foundation Stage: Assessment and Reporting Arrangements* (ARA). Standards and Testing Agency. Crown copyright. Available at: www.gov.uk/government/publications (accessed 21 September 2021).

Stewart, N. (2011) *How Children Learn: The Characteristics of Effective Learning*. St Albans: Early Education: The British Association for Early Childhood Education.

Taylor, F. *The Blank Language Scheme*. Available at: greatermanchester-ca.gov.uk/media/411511-the-blank-language-scheme-tip-5-questions-1901.pdf (accessed 21 September 2021).

CHAPTER 9

ON YOUR MARKS

Introduction

In Early Years settings there seems to be a great deal of focus on children being able to write and very little emphasis on the route that children need to take to be able to form recognisable letters. This is known as mark making – creating different patterns, lines and shapes using a variety of resources on a variety of textures and materials. Mark making can also refer to forms made with hands, paintbrushes, sticks, etc.

It is very important to note here that the term 'mark making' is not approved of by everyone in Early Years, as some people feel that it gives the impression that pictorial representation is inferior to early writing skills. That is not the case here, and I advocate equal value to pictorial representations and to marks that children consider 'their writing'.

This chapter will look at what mark making is and then consider why it is so important for children to be given lots of opportunities to experiment with marks. It will also consider all the different areas of development that mark making supports and how, and so the ways that we can encourage mark making will be discussed. It will then move on to something that we have had great success with in our setting, which is story scribing. This chapter will look at how to introduce story scribing and what we have learnt from our own experience with this in our setting.

What is mark making?

Learning to make marks is a process like any other and children need to be given the time and the opportunities to develop these skills and not be rushed into forming letters when they are not developmentally ready for it.

We all have a natural desire to express ourselves artistically, to leave something of ourselves for others to see. We all have a natural desire to communicate with each other by recording things that mean something to us. Children's attempts at this expression are the beginnings of recording and sharing, and representing their ideas graphically. Our response to these marks can influence how confident children will be in their abilities.

When children realise that marks can be used symbolically to carry meaning, in much the same way as the spoken word, they begin to use marks as tools to make their thinking visible. Mark making gives children the opportunity to express themselves and explore new materials other than pen and paper. The wonderful thing about mark making is that it is not just bound to the indoors – the outdoors affords plenty of exciting opportunities for children to explore the natural world and get mark making.

9.1 Two children mark making with chalk

Initially, when children start to experiment with making marks, it is a blend of writing and drawing as the children engage in the process and develop new skills. By the time children are 3 years old, most, but not all, will start to understand that there is a difference between writing and drawing, and may begin to role play different writing activities, especially if these have been modelled to them. Recently, two children were very busy playing outside and I observed that they were making marks on a small notepad. I could hear the conversation:

Child L: 'I'm writing my shopping list – got carrots, pineapple, cucumber, sweetcorn, tuna, cheese.'

Child J: 'Where will you go shopping?'

Child L: 'Hmm, don't know.'

I thought perhaps I could add something here to keep the play moving and I considered whether the children were aware of the name of some supermarkets, so I suggested, 'Well, maybe Tesco or Sainsbury's?'

Child L: 'Yes, Tesco. We need it for our dinner.'

This is an example of where children have observed the use of writing in everyday life, that writing actually has a purpose and makes sense to the children. It is crucial that, as Early Years Practitioners, we scaffold their learning of different activities where writing is used, that in this digital world children still see us writing.

Children, aided by adults, progress inside their own Zone of Proximal Development (Vygotsky, 1978) and gradually begin to master abilities that have not been developed until that moment, abilities such as scribbling. The adult's role in this process is vital: it is through the meaningful relationship that the child has established with the adults in the setting that graphical abilities can flourish and develop completely. The way we react to children's creations can make or destroy them and we must be mindful of this. If children see that we value these marks and scribbles and drawings, they will be encouraged to continue to express themselves. They will embrace creativity and gain confidence.

Giving the children in your settings the freedom to draw means that they can create anything they want. What they draw allows you to see what's going on in their mind, and also lets them grow in their uniqueness and originality. We can show interest by making comments about what they are drawing so that they feel good about their work and are more confident about themselves. Comments about the drawings may be better than questioning the children, as that can be stressful for some and comments allow the children to be able to chat about what the thinking process has been behind their wonderful creations.

For example, recently a child was busy drawing next to me and we just chatted about what she was doing, the colours she needed and she happily explained to me that she was drawing the planets and that we lived on the planet Earth. She told me about some of the other names of planets she knew and I was able to sprinkle some vocabulary over this by adding planet names. She then drew stars, giving me a commentary of her thought process. It was a truly lovely moment where she was able to demonstrate to me just how much knowledge she had.

Why is mark making so important?

Research has shown that mark making is crucial for a child's development and learning. Margaret Brooks explains how 'Through drawing [children] are not only able to see what they are thinking, they are also able to play around with and transform their ideas' (2009, p. 319). It not only teaches young children how to hold a pen correctly, but it also prepares them for writing and develops their handwriting skills.

When we are drawing, our imaginations are free to go anywhere and so for children, drawing is a wonderful way to increase and develop their imaginations without limitations. When children are imagining, they are able to form their own scenarios and play pretend. Encouraging imagination enables children to show freedom of expression and creativity, two major components I am sure we all agree that any child should have.

Creative development

Drawing is a very positive way for children to express their emotions. For all of us, some emotions are very powerful and overwhelming. Imagine being a young child who does not understand those emotions, cannot put them into words and does not yet realise that emotions are natural and perfectly normal. Drawing is a safe way for children to be able to express those powerful and potentially quite frightening emotions, and is a very positive outlet for them.

Mark making enables children to express themselves graphically and to create their own stories; it represents their thoughts and ideas. As they develop these creative skills, their marks become more complex and sophisticated, along with their developing language skills as they recite their stories to us.

Cognitive development

Through their drawings and marks, children demonstrate their thought processes and what they are feeling, so what they choose to draw, the patterns they use and the stories they portray, helps them build their knowledge and visual skills.

Mark making as a tool for thinking and learning

Mark making affords the young child the ability to symbolise meaning, play with ideas and make new connections. Children in Piaget's pre-operational stage of cognitive development will be using mark making to support their ability to remember (hold ideas in the mind) and to communicate those ideas with others and with themselves. Lev Vygotsky (1978) suggested that cognitive development is a social skill and shared with a More Knowledgeable Other (MKO) – someone who has a better understanding or a higher ability level than the learner, and this is with respect to a particular task, process or concept – to support those ideas. It is important to note here that the MKO does not have to be an adult, but can be other children. As Greg Bottrill says: 'Children are far better teachers than you and I will ever be' (2020, p. 44) – and we completely agree at pre-school.

By giving children the opportunity to explore different mediums of mark making, it engages them in sensory play and allows them to discover new exciting materials. This helps to enhance a child's critical thinking, brain development and language development, which gives them the ability to build towards more complex learning tasks in the future.

For example, last summer we had plenty of receptacles filled with water. Water, as we all know, is irresistible to children. The children not only played in this water but immersed themselves in it, which led to some children having soggy socks and they proceeded to make a pattern of footprints. There was much discussion about the sensation of the wet socks and the criss-cross patterns that were being made.

Physical development

When children are making these early marks and drawings, they are practising how to hold a pencil and control what they are doing with their muscles. This develops fine motor skills and hand–eye coordination. The development of holding a pencil correctly, in a pincer grip, will affect handwriting skills in the future.

In order to develop this control, children need to develop their gross motor skills, which involve the large muscles in arms, legs and torso. Mark making affords itself to large movements using arm muscles to design large-scale creations. The children in our setting really enjoy writing with chalk. Holding the chalk with the whole hand can really strengthen the palmar grasp. They also decided that they would 'paint the walls with water' using different size paint brushes. They enjoyed playing with this way of making marks and the freedom that allowed them to create on a bigger canvas. Giving the children in your setting plenty of opportunity to practise their physical movements will enable them to control their fine motor skills.

How can we encourage children to make marks?

As with most things, the environment is crucial. Are there plenty of opportunities for children to be able to draw, scribble and write around your setting? Are they able to access a variety of mediums and resources to be able to explore and develop their creativity? Are there opportunities for both small- and large-scale creations to develop and practise those necessary skills? Reflecting on these key questions at regular intervals is helpful because things change and our children's interests change. We always need to reflect on just how enabling our environments are.

9.2 Children mark making outside

It is perhaps not surprising to remember that children need to see the point of something. I don't know about you, but if I'm asked to draw or write something, my mind goes completely blank. If we are forcing our children to write because we need their name in a card, for example, or we need to write an observation about mark making, we are missing the point. That is of no interest or relevance to the child and there is a real danger that we will signal to them that writing is a chore, something that *has* to be done and is therefore not a lot of fun.

However, if children can see that writing has a reason for being done, a purpose, they want to write. I think it is important to reiterate here that it has to be purposeful to the children, not something that has purpose to us, the adults, and therefore has no meaning to the children. Going back to my example with the children making a shopping list, they knew that it had a purpose and so writing became an important part of their play.

We have been very inspired by Greg Bottrill and I was delighted to be able to attend his training session on the Message Centre. He states that 'Secret messages written on the things that children build or create is a highly engaging way of continuing that immersion in Mark Making'

(2020, p. 127). This is all about joy and bringing joy to writing, not for it to be a chore or an adult-directed activity. In our setting, we have found that the children have totally embraced the Message Centre. For example, last week we were chatting about where in the garden a fairy might sleep. One child discovered a hidden message among the plants and was convinced the fairies had left it for us. The children decided they would write messages in reply to the fairies. This engaged the children for a considerable amount of time, writing and hiding messages for the fairies to find. It was truly joyful.

In order to create an environment where children are actively engaged in making marks, it is key to ensure that the children have plenty of opportunities to express themselves graphically. Having an environment that is fully resourced with different types of medium in various areas will encourage the children to start putting their thoughts and imaginings on paper, walls, whiteboards, pavements and anywhere else appropriate. Valuing those marks empowers children and shows them that they have meaning and that writing is not a chore but has real purpose, and they have something to say. How wonderful is that!

I want to tell you a story: story scribing

We were inspired to take a closer look at story scribing after reading about Trisha Lee's *Helicopter Stories* (2016) based on the storytelling and story acting curriculum of Vivian Gussin Paley. During a *Helicopter Stories* session, children dictate their stories to an adult scribe. Later that same day, the class gather around a taped-out stage and the stories are acted out. The approach is suitable for children aged from 2 to 7 years.

In our setting, we liked the idea of scribing for the children. Our children are aged from 2 to 5 years. We don't expect them to be able to write a story yet, but once they get to school there will be more expectations on them to start to write. In the new EYFS Statutory Framework effective from September 2021, the Early Learning Goals for Writing are:

Children at the expected level of development will:

- Write recognisable letters, most of which are correctly formed.
- Spell words by identifying sounds in them and representing the sounds with a letter or letters.
- Write simple phrases and sentences that can be read by others.

So, by the end of Reception the expectation is there. If we can help to instil confidence in the child, with a love of storytelling, using their imagination, having a good vocabulary and an understanding of what a story is, this will undoubtedly help them when they get to school.

Introducing story scribing

We introduced story scribing in a very simple way. It can be really useful when reading a story to the children to routinely talk about the book, naming the front cover, back cover, the spine – explaining that we all have a spine too, which holds our body together and without it we would be a pile of jelly on the floor. The children will love this explanation, which will help them to remember that bit of the book. Talking about the characters, pointing out how the story starts and ends, and who wrote the book and who drew the pictures, really ensures that they become very familiar with these terms and learn what a story is. When we then invite them to tell us a story, they have an idea of what we are talking about. A good time to do this is during their focus week as part of the assessment of their progress. Usually, it is done during play and at a time when the adult thinks the child may have been sparked to write a story, such as having just told the adult about a painting or drawing they have done. If they do not want to tell you a story that is fine – there should be no pressure on them to do it. If they do, then that's great. We get the story scribing clipboard down and sit with them, preferably somewhere quiet. It is best to do this on a one-to-one basis, although you may find there is a queue waiting in the side-lines.

It is essential to record exactly what the child says word for word, regardless of the grammar, which demonstrates that you value their story. To start with, this is very often just a list of words, sometimes linked, sometimes just random words. It is important for the child to see the adult writing down their words. Gradually, over the months, the children begin to make real progress with their storytelling. It is a great assessment tool, showing progress in their imagination, their vocabulary, their understanding of the structure of a story, the characters. They move from a list of words to giving some real meaning to that group of words. Trisha Lee states that the children are then invited to draw an illustration to go with their story, so you can see progression in their drawing, their pencil control, their pencil grip and also an idea of their current interests.

Later, they can be invited to write their name if they are developmentally ready to do so, or maybe just their initial. Because you are taking the pressure off the child by removing any need for them to write, they are usually keen to write what they can.

It may be appropriate to invite the children to act out their story either at story time or at another time during the session, but we sometimes just leave it at story scribing. Acting out their story adds another dimension to their learning, but in a busy setting it can sometimes be difficult to manage. Instead of worrying that 'you are not doing it properly', concentrate on what is being achieved, such as using it as a 'teachable moment'. We always ask to keep a copy of the story for their folder as they want to take their story home. Wondering with the child how to copy their work can lead to discussions about using the photocopier. This is a great skill you can go through with them as, once taught, it is a skill they want to use again and again.

Recently, one of our 4-year-old girls was seen with another child offering to write his story for him during play. She can write her name well and was obviously very confident in her ability to offer to write for her friend. She wrote his story telling him, 'Don't worry, I can write it for you', giving him the reassurance we had previously given her. She wrote his story making marks on the paper left to right as if writing paragraphs. This was a lovely example of the confidence that story scribing can give a child to write.

A few things we have learnt while story scribing are:

- Make sure you write the child's story somewhere quiet away from the crowds, otherwise you are likely to get a lot of very similar stories, especially if the children are fairly young. We had a lot of stories just about cheese!
- Wait until the child is 3 years old before attempting story scribing so they have had time to experience a lot of stories being read to them first.
- Use an A5 size piece of paper or the story may be extremely long.
- Encourage parents to try this at home too.

By using story scribing and the Greg Bottrill's Message Centre, we are giving the children some great tools to use to support their mark making and story-telling skills without piling pressure on them to write. We have no problem in our setting getting children to mark make, so I think the strategy of not telling children they must sit down and write their name is working well. Do you use story scribing or is it a strategy you would consider introducing to your setting? You only need a piece of paper and a pen and your children's wonderful imaginations to make a start.

9.3 Child with 'message centre' outside

Learn more

In this chapter we have looked at mark making, why it is so important and how we can encourage children to mark make, and explored story scribing and how you could introduce it in your setting. If you want to learn more, I recommend the following website: www.canigoandplaynow.com where Greg Bottrill discusses the Message Centre, and *The Ultimate Guide to Mark Making in the Early Years* by Sue Cowley.

References

Bottrill, G. (2020) *School and the Magic of Children*. London: Sage.

Brooks, M. (2009) Drawing, visualisation and young children's exploration of 'big ideas'. *International Journal of Science Education*, 31(3), 319–141.

Cowley, S. (2019) *The Ultimate Guide to Mark Making in the Early Years*. Lutterworth: Featherstone Education.

Department for Education (2021) *Statutory Framework for the Early Years Foundation Stage*. DfE. Crown copyright. Available at: https://assets.publishing.service.gov.uk/government/uploads/system/uploads/attachment_data/file/974907/EYFS_framework_-_March_2021.pdf (accessed 21 September 2021).

Lee, T. (2016) *Princesses, Dragons and Helicopter Stories*. Oxford: Routledge.

Vygotsky, L.S. (1978) *Mind in Society: The Development of Higher Psychological Processes*. Cambridge, MA: Harvard University Press.

CHAPTER 10

THE JOY OF NURSERY RHYMES

Introduction

For anyone working with young children, nursery rhymes are part of a tool kit, an essential source of learning opportunities. They are used by practitioners to teach language development, new and sometimes strange vocabulary, different seasons, actions and finger movements to aid cognitive development to the sheer joy of using the voice to sing.

The sound of a nursery rhyme has a pattern and cadence similar to a conversation in English. The ups and downs and pauses experienced while repeating the memorised rhyme aloud gives children a patterned and predictable practice of these components of language. The musical sing-song rhythm has the power to entertain but also to comfort. Rhymes have a natural flow that is easy to share and remember. They rely on meter and rhyme to stay in our memories.

This chapter will look at the sounds and patterns of rhymes and how they are a part of our cultural heritage. It will look at how the singing of nursery rhymes is a fun and fantastic way to teach children a variety of skills. It will also discuss why nursery rhymes are an important part of an Early Years curriculum, and what our role is in encouraging and supporting the singing of rhymes.

Cultural heritage and a social experience

Nursery rhymes are part of our cultural heritage, passed down through generations linking the childhood of grandparents with their grandchildren. They connect us to other people, linking us to the past; they become part of a wider shared experience for young children. They are not only able to sing along with adults, but there is a moment when they realise that other people also know these rhymes too. This sense of being part of a group and being able to join in is an important step in growing up and interacting with others. Each retelling connects us to the past, present and future. Now, perhaps more than ever, connection is crucial.

The singing of nursery rhymes creates a social experience for both the children and adults, and a feeling of group togetherness and a real sense of belonging. It is a great opportunity for children to get to know the other children in your setting. Singing together, joining in with all the actions and holding hands during rhymes such as 'Row, Row, Row Your Boat' supports the development of those crucial social skills.

10.1 "Row, row, row your boat"

As children develop at different rates, using nursery rhymes will support their communication and language development at whatever stage they are – for example, older children may be beginning to learn to rhyme and rhyming words, whereas younger children may still be at the stage of learning new words. There is real joy for both the adult and child when any child joins in with a rhyme for the first time; some may only be able to manage some of the actions, but using Makaton alongside your rhymes will give them another way to join in. Makaton is a unique language programme originally devised in the early 1970s by Margaret Walker, a speech and language therapist. It was revised in 1996 for children and adults with a variety of communication and learning difficulties. It is a language programme using speech, signs and symbols which provide both basic communication and everyday vocabulary, helping to develop language and literacy skills. Used alongside verbal language, it is great not only for young children, but also for those with additional needs or those with English as an additional language, as well as for all the children in your setting. A child's speech underpins their ability to write. So many children today are showing delay in their communication skills and anything that we can do to support them can only help.

Using nursery rhymes as a teaching tool

Nursery rhymes are a fantastic way for children to learn the following skills:

- Auditory discrimination: the ability to recognise differences in sounds allows a person to tell the difference between words and sounds that are similar, as well as words and sounds that are different.
- Listening skills: children need to be able to listen (active listening) rather than just hear.
- A rich range of language: as discussed, nursery rhymes use complex vocabulary that the child may not be introduced to in normal conversation.
- Concentration skills: this is, of course, vital as children need to concentrate to learn oral storytelling/poetry skills. These skills will be useful as children advance through school.
- Phonemic awareness: this refers to the specific ability to focus on and manipulate individual sounds (phonemes) in spoken words. Phonemes are the smallest units comprising spoken language. Phonemes combine to form syllables and words. For example, the word 'mat' has three phonemes: /m/ /a/ /t/.

Nursery rhymes enable children to learn:

- to be able to listen for and keep a steady beat – you can support this by clapping, patting, stamping, etc. along with the beat so the children can join in with this and feel the beat;
- whole rhymes off by heart from a very young age – this happens in an enjoyable and fun way;
- to be able to retell and sing these independently – a Froebelian approach (Friedrich Froebel (Tovey, 2013) believed that songs and rhymes provided key learning experiences for children) to rhymes places emphasis on these being sung either by adults or children spontaneously and frequently in settings;
- to be able to complete a rhyming sentence or couplet by predicting the word that is missing – e.g. 'Hickory, dickory dock, the mouse ran up the . . . '

- to be able to discriminate rhyming words and identify those that don't rhyme;
- to make their own strings of rhymes during wordplay – e.g. cat/ fat/ mat/ sat/ hat/ bat;
- to invent and experiment with making their own 'silly' words that rhyme; during song time recently, on hearing the word 'spider', one of the boys turned to me and made up several nonsense rhyming words such as blider, fider, etc. He was so pleased when I laughed along with him.

Teaching children nursery rhymes will help them to be better readers later on in life. When singing nursery rhymes, we naturally speak more clearly and slowly than we normally would, which is a good way for children to learn the words and understand how they are formed. They also love to imitate you, so have fun with the songs by making funny faces and movements to match the words, and they will have lots of fun doing them with you.

Singing nursery rhymes and songs to children as young as babies can help develop their language and communication skills from an early age. There are so many different ways that adults can make this type of learning fun, whether this is by using props, music or musical instruments. Creating a fun experience for children will help engage them and they are more likely to sit and participate in the songs. It is important to remember that younger children will only sit for short periods of time; we don't expect them to sit for a half-hour song session and we also find that impromptu singing is something the children enjoy. For example, last week, after some chatting together one of the children started to sing 'Wind the bobbin up'. I joined in and soon a group of us were singing and doing the actions.

Introducing children to a variety of nursery rhymes can help them understand and learn about different sounds. This is an important part of developing those early literacy skills. Listening to different sounds in the environment as well as in nursery rhymes provides children with the foundations in helping them to read and write.

As nursery rhymes are fun and full of sounds, children will tune into these sounds. Older children will experiment in combining sounds and blend them together to form a word. It can be really useful to laminate the rhymes and have them in key places around the setting. There are so many nursery rhymes and often we start singing one and I just cannot remember the words. Being able to grab a copy is so helpful to spare my embarrassment. Having them laminated protects them and makes them last.

Children relish listening to songs full of rhyming, rhythm and repetition. By singing songs containing these core elements, it is helping to boost children's language, communications and literacy development. Understanding the full value of nursery rhymes and songs will open up the learning opportunities for children and help to create a positive attitude towards language.

Why is singing nursery rhymes and songs important?

In summary, singing nursery rhymes and songs is important for a number of reasons.

- Children learn new words.
- Children develop their non-verbal communications skills.
- Children learn early maths skills.
- Children understand how words are formed.
- It enables children to copy actions.
- It boosts children's language, communication and literacy skills.
- It helps to develop children's social skills.
- Children learn about different beats and rhythms.
- It provides the opportunity for children to value language and become confident learners.
- It creates a close relationship between adult and child.

The adult's role in singing nursery rhymes and songs

Confidence is key for us as staff. I have worked with many members of staff who are embarrassed to sing and feel foolish. This is not a talent show; the children don't have scores or red buzzers – they just enjoy the activity of singing together with an interested adult. If you are confident when singing nursery rhymes, this will be portrayed to the children, but perhaps more importantly, if the adults are having fun, children are more likely to respond.

In our setting, we have found the following techniques to be helpful for adults involved with singing nursery rhymes with children.

- **Sing songs slowly and clearly**. Children need to be able to hear the words and melody to join in. Some words in nursery rhymes, as I have said, are strange, unusual and unfamiliar, so the children really need to hear them so they can sing along and make sense of what they are singing. It is a great opportunity to chat about the words used.
- **Use props to support the songs**. We use a bag containing props such as a spider finger puppet, toy sheep, etc. to prompt the children, which we call the 'sing it bag'. The children love it and are so excited when the sing it bag comes out and we ponder together what might be in it that day. I always change what props are inside the bag to keep that element of surprise and excitement. It is very popular with the children and also with parents.

- **Involve children**. Encourage their interaction by enabling them to think of appropriate actions to the rhymes. Again, I always find their actions far better and more imaginative than mine. Also, if they have been involved in making those decisions, they are far more likely to remember the actions.
- **Five rhymes**. We plan which nursery rhymes we will focus on each term, which was recommended to us from an In The Moment Planning training session entitled Observe, Plan, Interact, Assess, Track we attended run by Early Years Training Surrey. We liked this idea as it enables us to really focus on those five elements and ensure that the children know them and can sing them independently. We put pictures of the rhymes on a board so that the children choose which rhymes we sing during a session. The idea is to choose five or six rhymes that cover various aspects of learning: we use a rhyme that teaches fine motor skills such as 'Incy Wincy Spider'; one that teaches gross motor skills, such as 'The Grand Old Duke of York'; a rhyme that teaches children to cross the midline such as 'Wind the Bobbin Up' (there are many rhymes that can be used to support crossing the midline, just make sure you move your arms and legs across your midline when demonstrating the actions), and usually two rhymes that work on numbers, '1, 2, 3, 4, 5, Once I Caught a Fish Alive', and perhaps one that counts down such as 'Rockets'. This is such a simple and effective way to teach all those key skills in a five minutes a day activity.

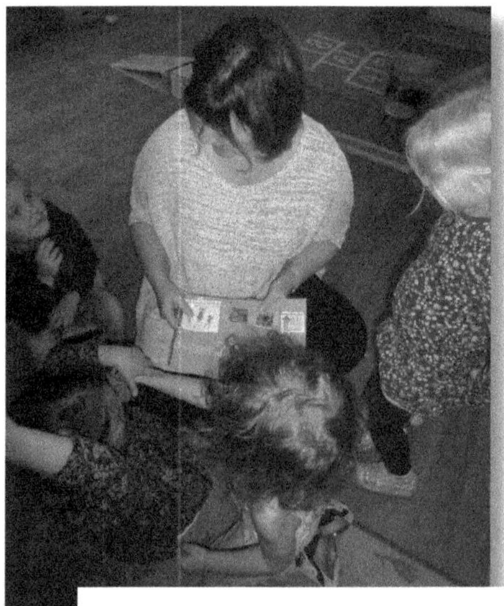

10.2 Dawn with children choosing rhymes

Is singing nursery rhymes and songs included in your everyday routine? Singing nursery rhymes doesn't just have to be during song time. Why not share a song or two during nappy time or when children are sitting down for lunch or while playing outside. These times are ideal in providing children with opportunities to develop their communication and language skills. There is nothing more wonderful than children bursting into spontaneous singing. Singing is fun and should be part of a rich Early Years, so relax and go for it – the children will love it!

Learn more

In this chapter we have looked at how nursery rhymes help children to learn about language and explored the adult's role in singing rhymes and songs and how nursery rhymes are part of a cultural heritage. If you are interested in learning more about nursery rhymes, I recommend checking the https://wordsforlife.org.uk website (accessed 20 July 2021) as they give ideas for activities.

Useful websites

www.makaton.org

www.pacey.org.uk/news-and-views/pacey-blog/october-2019/the-importance-of-nursery-rhymes-in-early-childhood/

https://theconversation.com/music-training-speeds-up-brain-development-in-children-61491

References

Tovey, H. (2013) *Bringing the Froebel Approach to your Early Years Practice*. Oxford: Routledge.

CHAPTER 11

MUD, GLORIOUS MUD: THE MUD KITCHEN

Introduction

Mud always seems to be a popular activity with young children. In our setting, the children's fascination with mud is not affected by the weather; they are happy in the mud come rain or shine. The children are also interested in the soil, the feeling of it running through their hands and they enjoy the way it looks, running around showing everyone their grubby hands. There is plenty of play in the soil, adding dinosaurs and various toy vehicles, but once water is added, excitement grows. The combination of mud and water creates opportunities for exploration, cooperative play and lots of sensory discovery. Mud play is all about fun, fun, fun. There is something endlessly joyful about jumping into a muddy puddle.

This chapter will discuss getting staff and parents on board with mud play, and will look at suitable clothing and expectations regarding cleaning up after playing. It will discuss how mud play is so open-ended and inclusive, and will explain why mud – although it can be messy – is actually good for you. Finally, it will suggest how you might set up your own mud kitchen.

Getting staff and parents on board

Mud isn't for every child – there are those children who are very uncomfortable getting themselves dirty, and there are many parents who are very uncomfortable with their children getting dirty and the possibility of clothing getting spoiled.

It may be that in your setting there will be practitioners who are not keen on this type of play and, of course, it does create mess. The most important thing is to understand their resistance, but to explain the benefits of allowing and embracing mud play. Share with your more reluctant staff and parents the advantages of having a mud kitchen and/or a mud pit. Clothes and resources will get dirty, so discussing together as a team how you will accommodate this would be useful to ensure that everyone is on board; explaining to parents when they come to visit your setting that you actively engage in mud play and that children need to dress accordingly will set the expectations right from the beginning. This will need to be discussed and agreed with parents. To really make for successful mud play, everyone has to be happy and to have agreed to your rules.

One approach, which we have found useful in helping parents and those more reluctant staff members to get on board with mud play, is to show them how much fun and learning can happen with mud. We post photos on our social media for parents; they cannot fail to see the absolute joy that children feel when exploring mud. We describe the learning in our photos and share in our weekly update. The children are excited to share their joy with their parents too, telling them of their exploits. On one occasion some of the children had become so muddy that we had to wash their feet and legs in a bowl of water and wash the mud from their hair. We used a hair dryer to dry their hair and this was an adventure in itself. They were so excited to tell their parents

Suitable clothing and expectations

Before the children begin to play, it is important to make sure they are wearing clothes that can become muddy. You can provide waterproof aprons, which are useful in sunnier weather to minimise the mess on clothes, but I would advise that children come to your setting with a set of waterproofs. One setting I know encourages children to have lined waterproofs for use during the winter and another set for the warmer weather. It's a good idea for children to wear rain boots while they are playing in the mud. Agree what your expectations are for the children regarding cleaning up after the play. Soapy water can be provided so that a routine is established of the children washing up resources, etc. after playing in the mud. From my experience, they enjoy this almost as much as the mud play. The children themselves may need cleaning too, so the best way to do this will also need to be discussed and agreed with your team. You may want to have a specific area that is to be used for changing out of muddy boots and then washing hands. This will make keeping your environment clean a lot easier as the mud stays in just the one area. If the rules are consistently followed and reinforced, the children soon get into a good habit and the mess can be minimised. Trying to keep boot changing, undressing out of waterproofs and hand washing outside and under cover is the ideal situation. Having some form of shelter keeps the children dry and not getting too cold as much as possible in inclement weather conditions.

We have used some of our Early Years Pupil Premium to purchase some high-quality waterproofs for children and they are then used for other children when they move on. We also have a collection of spare welly boots and waterproofs so all children can take part in this amazing activity.

11.1 Child with cup of mud soup

Open-ended and inclusive

The beauty of mud play is that it is so open-ended. There is no right or wrong way for the children to play with it; it has a never-ending range of opportunities for them to discover. Being so open-ended, it meets the diverse needs and interests of different children. They never seem to tire of playing in the mud, as I have observed play that has continued for the whole morning or afternoon session with so many components to that play. For example, we have a curry plant growing quite near to the mud pit, and once several boys were exploring mixing water into a large bowl of mud; one boy added some of the curry plant. 'I'm making curry,' he said. He asked me to smell his curry and we chatted about the smell. This caught the attention of the other boys; they began to get smaller bowls from the mud kitchen shed and started to concoct their own curries with much discussion about the texture of the curry and the strength of it, asking me at various points to smell their curry to test its strength.

Mud play is inclusive of all children as it allows them to play at their own developmental level and what feels comfortable for them. Younger or less skilled children might focus on the sensory experience, just enjoying exploring how it feels or simply wanting to dig; they can take it at their own pace. Older children may have more specific goals in mind for their mud play. I often observe them creating magic potions, making soup or even making me a cup of chocolate coffee. Some children may thoroughly enjoy the sensation of mud, while others are only comfortable poking a finger into it or just observing the play. Mud can be explored at their own comfort level. Remember, there are no right or wrong ways to play with mud – just their way.

There will be those children who are very happy to jump in muddy puddles, but there will be those who do not want to be so directly involved in the mud. This can be a very useful teachable moment to support those less keen children and to explain to others about respecting each other and that not everyone will want to get mud all over themselves. We can support children to enjoy jumping in the mud, but check first who is around and may get splashed.

Mud is good for you

Of course it is about the fun, but the really great news is that playing with mud is good for our children – it has lots of benefits. Mud is dirty and it makes the children dirty. As discussed earlier, this can be problematic for settings and make practitioners feel very uncomfortable. It's time-consuming getting the children ready to play in the mud – wet-weather gear, wellies, etc. – and time-consuming getting them cleaned up afterwards. Parents may well not be happy with the idea of their children digging in the mud at nursery or pre-school. This is where knowing about the wonderful benefits of playing in the mud can really strengthen your case.

Scientists have now confirmed something that children have somehow always known: playing in mud is a joyful and fun experience. Research by Lowry et al. (2007) has shown that dirt contains microscopic bacteria called Mycobacterium vaccae which stimulates the immune system and increases the levels of serotonin in our brains, soothing and calming children and helping them to relax. I have found that increasingly children have less time to relax with the result that anxiety is on the rise; mud play is an easy way to counter that. Children are able to squeeze it, pat it, run it through their fingers and just get their hands into it. This sort of malleable and sensory play can be very soothing. The above research shows that regular exposure to the bacteria may help reduce a child's vulnerability to depression, something that is becoming a real cause for concern in Early Years, and we all want that. Yes, mud is dirty but it makes us happy.

Playing with mud gives children a real, hands-on sense of the earth, which is crucial if we want them to have an appreciation for their environment and develop a desire to take care of it. This can be explained to parents so they can really understand the many positives there are in playing with mud.

Setting up a mud kitchen

So, how do you go about setting up a mud kitchen? If this is something you are considering, this is how we went about it. We knew we wanted to have a mud kitchen and already had a mud pit which the children really loved. We understood that mud is a fantastic open-ended resource with so many learning opportunities and we wanted to explore this. Greg Bottrill (2018) states that a mud kitchen 'lends itself to connecting children to the natural world'. In our experience, children spend a lot of time in the mud kitchen showing high levels of involvement and use it in all weathers.

Our mud pit originally was just a wooden raised bed filled with topsoil. Initially, we had a plastic kitchen that had been given to us which children used alongside the mud pit. We planned to change it to a wooden one when we could afford it, as we wanted to adhere to the ethos of authentic and sustainable resources. Our children all loved the mud and we allowed them to access the nearby water as they wanted to. There really is no point having a mud kitchen unless you are prepared to allow the children access to water. We provided them with lots of real pots and pans, wooden and metal utensils, hand whisks, enamel mugs, plastic cups and plates, a wooden pestle and mortar. We had plants nearby, including the curry plant and lots of natural resources for them to add to their play.

Our mud kitchen has evolved over time and after reflecting on how the children were using it and what we wanted from it, we now have a wooden mud kitchen. We discussed with the children what different types of resources they might like to use in the mud kitchen and explained to them that we would need to save up some money in order to buy these. Eventually, we were able to buy a variety of resources to be used in the mud kitchen. Alongside it we now have tables and chairs to serve their cooking to others, as well as buckets and large pans to mix and stir their concoctions.

The water is now in a large barrel which they can access with a little help. It sits in a tray, so any spilled water can be used by spooning or scooping it up and transporting it to where they want to play with it. Again, this links to children caring for their environment and developing an understanding of sustainability. We use this as a teachable moment for children to appreciate how to save water and use it carefully.

If you want to introduce a mud kitchen, just do it. It doesn't have to be big or fancy. It just needs the basics: access to mud, water and kitchen tools.

It may be pertinent to place it away from the sand, otherwise the children will mix the two. It will be up to you to give the children some simple boundaries and then step back and watch their fun and learning. Where would you place your mud kitchen?

Mud enables children to connect to nature, which embraces the approach of one of my favourite pioneers of play, Friedrich Froebel (1782–1852). A key Froebelian principle is that everyday experience of the natural world is essential for children to learn about the beauty of nature and how it relates to all living things. We are all keen to encourage our children to appreciate the world around them and develop a love for their environment. Playing in the mud supports this love. By providing time for the children to be outdoors, experience nature and the chance to engage in muddy, messy play, we will be encouraging the next generation to take care of our world.

11.2 Children playing with mud

Learn more

In this chapter we have looked at how to encourage staff and parents to feel positive about mud play and embrace the joy of it. We have explored suitable clothing and how to set up a mud kitchen in your setting. If you would like to learn more about mud, I suggest *50 Fantastic Ideas for Things to do with Mud and Clay* by Judit Horvath. The following website provides plenty of ideas and useful information: https://muddyfaces.co.uk/outdoor-hub/mud/shop-mud-kit.

References

Bottrill, G. (2018) *Can I Go & Play Now?* London: Sage.

Horvath, J. (2017) *50 Fantastic Ideas for Things to do with Mud and Clay*. London and New York: Featherstone Education.

Lowry et al. (2007) Identification of an immune-responsive mesolimbocortical serotonergic system: Potential role in regulation of emotional behavior. *Neuroscience*, 146(2–5): 756–72. doi: 10.1016/j.neuroscience.2007.01-067. Available at: www.ncbi.nlm.nih.gov/pmc/articles/PMC1868963/ (accessed 22 September 2021).

CHAPTER 12

MATHS IS EVERYWHERE

Introduction

Many of us are frightened of maths. Our memories of it from our own childhood can be traumatic and it fills us with dread and anxiety. Over the years, many practitioners that I have worked with have shied away from maths activities with children and any interaction that could involve maths, so we tend to stay with a very basic, narrow view of maths, usually concerned with asking questions about numbers, shapes or colours. The EYFS outcome for numeracy is one of the top areas where children are not achieving. This is a worrying trend.

This chapter will discuss how we need to change attitudes to maths and instead instil children with a positive attitude to the subject. The chapter will look at how child-initiated play is fundamental to children being able to engage in mathematical thinking. It will also explore the different ways that children learn maths, such as number sense, representation, spatial sense, measurement, patterns and problem-solving.

Being positive about maths

'Being bad at maths' is a very common saying and attitude. It doesn't seem to be an attitude that concerns us. It is almost socially acceptable and this perhaps leads all of us into perpetuating a lack of confidence and competence regarding mathematics with our youngest children. We therefore need to be positive about maths around children and to model the attitude that maths is important and that it is possible for everyone to develop good mathematical skills. We need to equip our children with a can-do attitude regarding maths.

Learning about maths begins from birth as children explore the world around them. As they develop, they are supported in their learning by the people around them. The environment is a rich resource for engaging with mathematics, especially when it provides opportunities to listen to and use mathematical language, and to engage in mathematics with everyday experiences. With encouragement and guidance from us, we can draw children's attention and activities in ways that enable them to reason and grow in their abilities to communicate mathematically. As they do so, they develop an affinity with mathematical tools, and they take pleasure and interest in thinking mathematically. We need to instil a sense of joy in maths. If we react positively in situations where maths can be explored, the children will take this joy throughout their school life and beyond.

For children, however, maths is not something separate from any other area of learning – we know their learning is holistic in nature. Using mathematical language can be developed most appropriately when children have the opportunities to practise in contexts that are not specifically mathematical.

12.1 Boys lining up

Child-initiated play and maths

A lack of child-initiated play severely limits possibilities for children to explore and communicate their own interests and mathematical ideas. It also restricts opportunities for children to engage in the sort of dialogue that can scaffold their understanding about their graphical marks and symbols, limiting their mathematical thinking and communication. Genuine child-initiated play is spontaneous and belongs to the child or children; it is not imposed by adults with a maths agenda. Maths needs to have personal meaning for children and to be deeply rooted in their play. They learn mathematical skills through their daily experiences and the more meaningful it is to them, the better. It should not be about checklists and never-ending questions. As Greg Bottrill (2018, p. 89) states: 'Mathematics through play enables it to be free from restrictions and, above all, it becomes something joyful.'

Ensuring that your environment, inside and out, is full of mathematical opportunities and has exciting things for children to explore, sort, compare, count, calculate and describe, enables children to be creative, critical thinkers, problem solvers and to have a go, developing that can-do attitude mentioned earlier. I have often observed that hot spots for maths chat are rarely in areas set up for maths. Interestingly, maths chat happens everywhere else – for example, in the mud kitchen where children sort and categorise receptacles appropriate for creating concoctions.

12.2 Child making cup cakes

Allowing children to make mistakes is also crucial for mathematical development. If they don't make mistakes, they won't be learning, and making errors can show practitioners what the children are thinking, and they can then give them the required support. We tend not to want children to make mistakes and then jump in too early, so we need to learn to resist this.

One of the key methods that children use to learn is trial and error. Therefore, using a hands-on approach and allowing them to experiment is a good way for children to develop their mathematical thinking skills. Knowing when to intervene or not when children are heading for mistakes is crucial, as voicing what they are thinking can help children to identify the inconsistencies in their understanding of something, as discussed in Chapter 6: to intervene or not to intervene, that is the question.

The theory behind mathematical thinking

Early years pioneers Jerome Bruner and Jean Piaget advocated physical exploration that helps children to develop understanding of basic concepts. They believed that children internalise the knowledge they gain through hands-on experience and this later leads to more complex abstract thought. This theory is supported by the hugely influential Researching Effective Pedagogy in the Early Years (REPEY) and Effective Provision of Pre-school Education (EPPE) research projects, which advocate planning practical experiences for children to 'actively construct conceptual knowledge' (Siraj-Blatchford et al., 2002) through a balance of taught and 'freely chosen yet potentially instructive child-initiated activities' (Siraj-Blatchford et al., 2004).

Vygotsky (1978) discussed the role that social interaction has on children's learning, maintaining that children extend and consolidate their learning through dialogue with more knowledgeable others, whether adults or peers. The REPEY and EPPE research also supports this view as they identified the need for good, high-quality verbal interactions that extend and develop children's thinking.

How do children learn maths?

Children learn maths in a variety of ways, which we will now explore in more detail.

Number sense

This is the ability to count accurately, forwards initially, and then later children will learn to count backwards. A more complex skill related to number sense is the ability to see relationships between numbers – for example, adding and subtracting.

Stories, books, songs and nursery rhymes are a fantastic way to consolidate children's number sense. Having to think about numbers in the correct order takes a lot of effort and practice – it is much easier for children to do this through songs and rhymes and, perhaps more importantly, it is fun and maths needs to be fun. During these sessions give children time to talk, play and practise using numbers. Using your fingers or having objects that the children can see and touch will help too.

Gardner (1993, p. 76) states that children around the age of four are beginning and wanting to count everything. He describes that children at this stage of development are 'looking everywhere for evidence of numbers'. Daily routines like preparing snacks lend themselves to the development of mathematical learning and skills. Fruit can be halved or quartered, enabling discussions about how many pieces of fruit there are and whether there is enough for everyone. This makes maths concrete and of practical purpose for children.

Representation

Representation means making mathematical ideas 'real' by using words, pictures, symbols and objects (like blocks). It is useful to remember that children's mathematical development does not progress in a straight line. It may appear that they have achieved and made a breakthrough in their thinking, but they suddenly revert back to their earlier understandings, and making these ideas real may well support their thinking. Real-life experiences are required to extend and develop children's understanding of the world and such experiences are rich in mathematical potential.

Being able to compare quantities by looking at sets of objects and deciding which is larger or smaller is the very early stages of calculating. During this type of play, children can start to learn the vocabulary associated with it, such as more, less and the same; as they add more objects, they can practise the concept of multiplication. If objects are taken away, they can experiment with subtraction. Snack time provides a great opportunity to sort different fruits, etc. on to plates, comparing them using the senses such as look and smell, and deciding whether the pieces are bigger or smaller than each other. The outside area also provides some wonderful natural opportunities to calculate. We have strawberries growing at the moment: how many do we have? The children can discuss if we have more or less ripe strawberries than the week before; they also love to find acorns in the autumn months and can calculate who has more or less.

Spatial sense

Later in school, children will call this 'geometry', but for toddlers it is introducing the ideas of shape, size, space, position, direction and movement.

Froebel understood the importance of teaching the idea of the interconnectedness of objects. He designed solid three-dimensional shapes which are called 'Froebel's Gifts'. Froebel intended children to explore the idea of a relationship between the part and the whole. Children explore mathematical and scientific concepts (such as number and shape) through direct manipulation of physical objects. As children build and experiment with such objects they develop richer ways of thinking about mathematical concepts such as number, size and shape. The Froebel block play research project (Bruce and Gura, 1987–90) has continued Froebel's work and the purpose was to show the development of the child's understanding of competence in controlling the dimensional shapes.

Babies learn about space, shape and size through mouthing, handling and exploring objects. Older children are more likely to understand mathematical concepts like position and size if they are able to use their body movements and senses to feel what it's like to be in, on or under something.

Measurement

Measuring involves finding the length, height and weight of an object using units such as millimetres, centimetres or metres. For children, it is a much more practical concept and draws heavily on their day-to-day activities. Measurement of time also falls under this skill area. Visual timetables are a really useful way to sequence the order of routines and time. Again, real-life experiences consolidate learning, and cooking lends itself beautifully to measuring. Scientific concepts can be explored and plenty of maths vocabulary can be worked on. It is a great sensory experience and can also develop small and fine motor skills. Cooking includes capacity, volume and estimation. Snack time can also provide opportunities, as children can measure capacity when pouring drinks and check to see whether there are enough chairs or cups for everyone and whether you need to take some away.

12.3 Child measuring

Patterns

Patterns are things – numbers, shapes, images – that repeat in a logical way. Patterns help children learn to make predictions, to understand what comes next, to make logical connections and to use reasoning skills. It is worth noting that patterns don't only occur in mathematics, but in many other areas such as the natural world, music and art. These areas can be explored to consolidate children's understanding of patterns in a very practical and creative way. Discovering nature in the outside area can support this: ladybirds and butterflies are fascinating to children and their patterns can be discussed and spots counted. We often find that children are very keen to discover how they can explore symmetry and we provide creative opportunities to make their own butterfly pictures by folding the paper to have symmetrical wings. Small world play with animals can lead to chatting about their patterns, stripes, spots, and so on, and why they have these patterns.

Problem solving

Problem solving is the ability to think through a problem and to recognise that there is more than one path to the answer. It means using past knowledge and logical thinking skills to find an answer. Being playful and creative are useful when problem solving – the thinking process involved in play is vital for the development of mathematical thinking to support problem solving. Children need to be encouraged to offer explanations to each other and accept everyone's contributions, which is not easy and needs plenty of practice. We are careful not to step in and give solutions, but rather encourage the children to find their own way by wondering what we could do in the situation. If that does not work, then it is critical to stay supportive and offer guidance so they can try again with another idea.

Conclusion

Maths is everywhere, in all aspects of our lives; it touches us every day. Yet for many of us, maths is something to fear and avoid. For young children, maths is an exciting part of their lives, it offers so many opportunities to explore, discover and to enjoy. We need to harness this attitude and encourage these skills so our children can feel confident and enthusiastic about all things relating to maths. This can best be achieved through rich, child-initiated play and an environment where maths is valued and supported.

Learn more

In this chapter we looked at having a positive attitude to maths and discussed how child-led play leads to rich opportunities for maths discovery. We explored how children learn maths in a variety of ways. For further information, please visit the website Karen Wilding Education (https://karenwildingeducation.co.uk). For further reading on maths, I recommend *Messy Maths: A Playful, Outdoor Approach for Early Years* by Juliet Robertson.

References

Bottrill, G. (2018) *Can I Go & Play Now?* London: Sage.

Gardner, H. (1993) *The Unschooled Mind*. London: Fontana.

Robertson, J. (2017) *Messy Maths: A Playful Outdoor Approach for Early Years*. Bancyfelin: Independent Thinking Press.

Siraj-Blatchford et al. (2002) *Researching Effective Pedagogy in the Early Years*. Available at http://www.327matters.org/docs/rr356.pdf

Siraj-Blatchford et al. (2004) *The Effective Provision of Pre-School Education (EPPE) Project*. Available at http://dera.ioe.ac.uk/8543/7/SSU-SF-2004-01.pdf

Vygotsky, L.S. (1978) *Mind in Society: The Development of Higher Psychological Processes*. Cambridge, MA: Harvard University Press.

CHAPTER 13

PLAY PARTNERS

Introduction

Now more than ever we need to be advocating the benefits of play and a play-based curriculum in the Early Years. By play, I refer to child-led play, freely chosen by that child or children and under their control. If the play is freely chosen by the children, you may think, what role do I have in this? As a play partner! No promises here, being a play partner sounds easy, but it takes knowledge and skill, and learning to be a play partner does require patience. The key is to be interested in the child and what the child is actively trying to achieve in their play. It is crucial not to be consumed by outcomes or worrying about what the purpose is – children know the purpose of their play; we just need to spend the time to find out. The child is able to choose the purpose and therefore the learning potential at exactly the right level of understanding for them.

This chapter will discuss being a play partner and what that involves, including sensitive interactions between adults and children. It will consider the use of questions in play to make sure we get the balance right to ensure that we are able to develop strong, emotional relationships with our children.

Being a play partner

A play partner is able to respond to and follow a child's lead. This means that the child is able to stay in control of the play, but enjoy the company of adults. While the adults may make suggestions or bring additional resources or provocations to the play, the adult follows what the child is interested in, playing a supportive role.

Being a play partner can be especially important when working with very young children. It can encourage communication and language skills. It is the perfect opportunity to model language skills, new and interesting vocabulary and ways of communicating, including the rules of communication.

Children are very astute. They instinctively know when an adult is genuinely interested in them and what they are doing. They will often choose you to be a part of their play. If you engage with them, are open and interested and playful, they will come to you. If the child initiates the interaction, then you can feel assured that this is the child's decision, their choice and so something they are invested and interested in.

To truly engage as a play partner, the adult needs to focus on the child, put that child at the centre of what is being said and what is happening right there in that moment, not focusing on outcomes. Learning and next steps will occur quite naturally and as you are part of the play, you will be attuned to those and respond immediately when it has the most meaning to that child.

Children appreciate a playful adult, one that shows enthusiasm, being ready to follow the child's responses. Being a play partner enables children to feel secure and develop independence. Playing with children can encourage them to have a sense of self-efficacy – i.e. making decisions for themselves. Child-initiated play gives children the opportunity to make their own choices. Greg Bottrill reminds us that if we engage in the play, we will not be pulling children away from play, 'Instead, you are being pulled into children's play' (2018, p. 49).

13.1 Debra and child

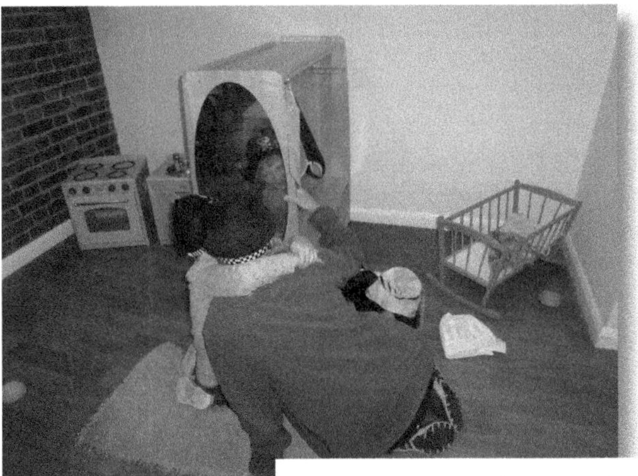

13.2 Debra playing with children

Sensitive interactions

Being an effective play partner requires sensitive interactions where you will be deciding if questions are appropriate in the situation. It can sometimes be better to actually be the one answering the children's questions rather than asking them. When adults interact sensitively with children during their play, they can support children's language skills. It is the perfect opportunity to sprinkle those skills over the top of the play. Part of being sensitive to the children is to make sure that you are noticing what is engaging them and deciding your role – not noticing and therefore not offering any support is very different from allowing the children to keep control of their play.

Getting the balance of questions right is crucial. It is key not to ask too many questions or interrupt the child's thoughts. All interactions start with chat. Through chatting with the children, they understand that we are interested in what they have to say and tell us. We can begin to build strong, emotional connections. We need to ensure that we are giving the children the time and the space to chat – with each other, not just with us. As Greg Bottrill says: 'child chat will often be far richer and interesting to the child than yours' (2018, p. 57).

Chatting with children

Chatting with children is not just about talking. Listening, *really* listening, to a child shows them that you are someone who is interested, who cares what they have to say. Child–adult relationships that are responsive and attentive – with lots of back-and-forth interactions – build a strong foundation in a child's brain for all future learning and development. This is called the serve-and-return effect. It is imperative to take turns and wait – don't rush to fill a pause, which could just be thinking and processing time for the child – but you want to keep the interaction going back and forth. Supporting and encouraging rewards a child's interests and curiosity, as never getting a return can actually be stressful for a child. When you return a serve, children know that their thoughts and feelings are heard and understood. Serve-and-return interactions shape the brain. When a child makes an attempt at communication, and an adult responds appropriately with eye contact, words or a gesture, neural connections are built and strengthened in the child's brain that support the development of communication, social and emotional skills.

13.3 Dawn with children

Creating conditions for rich language to occur through chatting with the children is part of having an enabling environment. Allowing children the space to chat to each other and where appropriate we the adults join and talk, adding and extending language, all happens during play and as we become partners in that play.

Timing

It is all too easy to dominate by hurrying children up, giving solutions to problems before they have tried out ideas or taking over their play in unhelpful ways. Sensitive interaction is about supporting and extending the play in ways that are appropriate to the children. Playing in parallel alongside a child and putting actions into words can be beneficial. For example, I remember an incident when I locked myself in the toilet and couldn't get out for ages. When I was finally rescued, I thought the children would have wondered where I had been and be really interested in my adventure. I was very keen to chat about it, but the children were far too busy chatting to each other and found my story rather dull. I had judged the timing wrong. A bit later they found it hilarious and were telling each other how I'd been stuck in the toilet! Timing and gauging reactions is part of having sensitive interactions with the children and this, of course, happens through developing strong relationships with them.

To ensure sensitive interactions, remember, too many questions can be stressful for children, so consider if a question is actually appropriate and that all interactions start with chat. Chatting with children enables rich language to happen and the best time for this is during play. Children respond well to playful adults – those adults who want to join in with their play, remembering, of course, not to dominate that play – and sensitive interactions, following the child's lead. However, we need to be aware of timing. Sensitive interactions can only happen if we give children time.

Strong, supportive relationships

When working with children, we want to develop really strong, supportive relationships. This means that the adults have to observe children's reactions and be responsive at that moment. The children will have the control to decide whether to invite you into their play or whether they do not actually need or want adult company. We must respond appropriately. Being emotionally available for those children enables strong, supportive relationships to flourish and demonstrates to the children that you are willing to engage with their play, but you will also not intrude upon their play. It also means deciding to move away if you can see that you are not required. There will always be other children who will benefit from the attention of the adult. I know some of us worry that if we are not always engaging with the children we are not doing our job properly, but then we can spoil play by taking part when we are not required, just because we think we should, so we need to be sensitive to our children and their needs.

Higher level thinking

Being a play partner enables us to encourage higher level thinking in the children. Through their play we start to develop and extend their thinking and learning. In being really engaged as a play partner with the children, we can draw their attention to certain features of what they are doing. It is possible for us to create opportunities that prompt interesting conversations and this can help children to think, explain and reason. The skill is to engage children and encourage the development of their thinking and learning without spoiling their enjoyment of their play. We should be carefully monitoring their responses to check if they are actually interested and want us there.

Standing back

Adults need to decide if their presence is needed in the child's play. Greg Bottrill (2018, p. 98) suggests taking time, observing the play and making a judgement:

> *there is no negativity in standing back and observing first, and then drink in the situation, the nowness of what is before you. By rushing in you can potentially extinguish play so that children then cease and look elsewhere within the setting to play, or you can end up imposing the direction of where the play leads.*

Children who are constantly playing with or using resources in the same way may not be expanding their learning and we cannot always assume that because they are playing, they are learning or developing their potential to continue to learn. Here is where the Leuven scales of involvement can support your decision making as to whether you are required as a play partner and can sensitively enhance the play to ensure learning potential is being met. You will have observed and assessed that you could model play, spark ideas about the play and then extend those ideas, perhaps by adding characters, scenarios and props, and encourage cooperation with peers.

Sustained shared thinking

The concept of 'partner' links closely to sustained shared thinking (SST). It is crucial for us to support children with their thinking and enable them to make sense of their world, and this is where sustained shared thinking can be valuable (Brodie, 2014). Time is needed to think and reflect on their play and the collaboration of SST can really foster children's learning. This play partnership between adults and children is very firmly in the tradition of Vygotsky and his belief in the role of the adult, guiding and supporting a child's learning. It can have real implications for settings, as having high engagement with children in their play can create deeper understanding of them, creating strong, supportive relationships. That emotional connection between the adult and the child is such a fundamental part of my pedagogy.

Being an effective play partner

By getting involved in children's play, there is a danger of the play becoming adult influenced, that the adult takes control. Being a true play partner can have a very positive impact on children's engagement, but it can also cause the play to disintegrate. Bryce-Clegg states:

> *judging if, when and how you intervene in children's play is not an exact science and no one gets it right all of the time. But, when you do it well, it allows you to observe, challenge, support and extend children's learning all based on the high-level engagement that you will get because they are at play.* (2015, p. 43)

Through being a play partner, adults can respond as appropriate – by responding to children in the moment, we will be able to spot a teachable moment. This will help the child to make progress.

Anna Ephgrave discusses the idea of pondering with children. Using phrases such as 'I wonder how . . . ?' or 'I wonder why . . . ?' shows the children that you do not have all the answers and that they have a say too. As Ephgrave states, this allows the child time to respond if they wish, tells the child that the adult is genuinely interested and that the adult does not know everything, and encourages the child to think back to supporting those higher level skills (2018, p. 98). I love to ponder with children and I find it works brilliantly, encouraging them to really think and ponder themselves. There is no stress or pressure as there is no right or wrong answer. The child is relaxed, engaged and supported, and so is learning.

Being an effective play partner means listening to children so the adult can build on what the child has to say. The Reggio Emilia approach discusses listening to children (www.reggiochildren.it). This discusses sensitivity to the patterns that connect us to others, a time full of silences, of long pauses – some adults feel that they need to fill the silences, sometimes with questions, thinking this is supporting the child's language development. Sometimes children need the silences to think, to process what is being said or what is happening. The adult filling that space stops this thinking process and the child has to go right back to the beginning. Tuning into the child enables an emotionally supportive relationship to flourish.

The beauty of being available as a play partner is that it is so much fun. I didn't get involved in teaching to stand around with a clipboard desperately writing observations and stressing about outcomes. I became an Early Years teacher to be with children. Sadly, the obsession with outcomes and other buzzwords such as school readiness and now catching up, means that we can forget that we are actually there for the children, to be present for those children. The only way to be present is to be available, and willing and excited to engage with those children. They deserve to be surrounded by adults who are ready to join in with their play and who want to have fun with them. How joyful!

Learn more

In this chapter we have looked at being a play partner and explored sensitive interactions and developing strong, supportive relationships with children. If you would like to learn more about being a play partner, I recommend Greg Bottrill's website, which you can find at www.canigoandplaynow.org.

References

Bottrill, G. (2018) *Can I Go & Play Now?* London: Sage.

Brodie, K. (2014) *Sustained Shared Thinking in the Early Years: Linking Theory to Practice*. Oxford: Routledge.

Bryce-Clegg, A. (2015) *Best Practice in Early Years*. London: Bloomsbury.

Ephgrave, A. (2018) *Planning in the Moment with Young Children: A Practical Guide for Early Years Practitioners and Parents*. Oxford: Routledge.

APPENDIX 1

TERMLY STANDARDISATION OF A CHILD'S FOLDER

Staff name:	**Date:**	**Date:**	**Date:**
Early Years Foundation Stage front sheet present			
Name of child recorded			
Start date of child recorded			
Age of child recorded in months throughout folder			
'One Page Profile' in folder			
Parent 'Focus Week' information and child photos in folder – with child comments			
Learning Journey summary completed termly and shared with parent/carer – copy to parent			
Focus points decided with parents/carers and recorded on Learning Journey			

(Continued)

(Continued)

Staff name:	**Date:**	**Date:**	**Date:**
Progress Tracking Form completed termly/accurately and shared with parent/carer			
2-year-old check completed if necessary and shared with parent/carer			
Samples/photos/wow moments/story scribing/ dated dd/mm/yy			
Evidence of progression of child's learning is visible			
Teachable moments are relevant and written up correctly			
ECAT assessment form completed when child starts then termly if necessary			
Blank level completed when child is 3 years old (during free play), then termly if necessary			
Signature (Supervisor)			

Comments:

APPENDIX 2

FORMAT FOR FEEDBACK AFTER FOCUS CHILD WEEK

- When you give the parent/carer the initial child focus week sheet, try and book an appointment with the parent for feedback the following week.
- Feedback meeting:

  1. Give the parent the summary to read or read to them/email to them.
  2. Show parent the child's focus week sheets and photos.
  3. Show them where the child is on the tracker – highlight areas working above and below, but more importantly point out the progress that has been made.
  4. Ask parent if they have any questions/concerns – record on the sheet.
  5. Discuss together the areas to focus on going forward – record on summary.
  6. Photocopy summary for parent.

- Feedback of 2-year check.

Use the same format as above but ask parent to place the 2-year check in the child's Red Book. If you have concerns about the child's development, discuss with parent and ask them to share the 2-year check with the HV. Discuss with SENCO.

APPENDIX 3

LEUVEN SCALES

Using the assessment of well-being and involvement scales

Laevers has created a five-point scale to measure both well-being and involvement. If there is a consistent low level of well-being and/or involvement, it is likely that a child's development will be threatened. The higher the levels of well-being and involvement we can achieve for the child, the more we can add to the child's development. When there are high levels of well-being and involvement, we know that deep-level learning is taking place.

The evaluation starts with assessing the levels of well-being and involvement using the tables. The procedure is simple and can be compared to 'scanning'. Observe the children individually or as a group for about two minutes then give a score for well-being and/or involvement using the five-point scale. Unless children are operating at level 4 or 5, learning will be limited. It is unrealistic to suggest that children will be operating at level 4 or 5 all of the time, as levels will fluctuate throughout the day.

However, it is useful to observe how well practitioners tune into the children's levels of well-being and involvement and respond to low levels sensitively. Even a low level of well-being or involvement can become a learning opportunity, which can result in higher levels.

(Ref: Well-being and Involvement in Care Settings. A Process-oriented Self-evaluation Instrument, Ferre Laevers (ed.) Research Centre for Experiential Education, Leuven University.

The Leuven scale for well-being

Level 1: Extremely low

The child clearly shows signs of discomfort such as crying or screaming. They may look dejected, sad, frightened or angry. The child does not respond to the environment, avoids contact and is withdrawn. The child may behave aggressively, hurting him/herself or others.

Level 2: Low

The posture, facial expression and actions indicate that the child does not feel at ease. However, the signals are less explicit than under level 1 or the sense of discomfort is not expressed the whole time.

Level 3: Moderate

The child has a neutral posture. Facial expression and posture show little or no emotion. There are no signs indicating sadness or pleasure, comfort or discomfort.

Level 4: High

The child shows obvious signs of satisfaction (as listed under level 5). However, these signals are not constantly present with the same intensity.

Level 5: Extremely high

The child looks happy and cheerful, smiles, cries out with pleasure. They may be lively and full of energy. Actions can be spontaneous and expressive. The child may talk to him/herself, play with sounds, hum, sing. The child appears relaxed and does not show any signs of stress or tension. He/she is open and accessible to the environment. The child expresses self-confidence and self-assurance.

The Leuven scale for involvement

Level 1: Extremely low

Activity is simple, repetitive and passive. The child seems absent and displays no energy. They may stare into space or look around to see what others are doing.

Level 2: Low

Frequently interrupted activity. The child will be engaged in the activity for some of the time they are observed, but there will be moments of non-activity when they will stare into space, or be distracted by what is going on around.

Level 3: Moderate

Mainly continuous activity. The child is busy with the activity but at a fairly routine level and there are few signs of real involvement. They make some progress with what they are doing but don't show much energy and concentration and can be easily distracted.

Level 4: High

Continuous activity with intense moments. The child's activity has intense moments and at all times they seem involved. They are not easily distracted.

Level 5: Extremely high

The child shows continuous and intense activity revealing the greatest involvement. They are concentrated, creative, energetic and persistent throughout nearly all the observed period.

APPENDIX 4

BLANK LEVEL QUESTIONS

The Very Hungry Caterpillar

Name:
Date:

	Level of question
[Pages 1 & 2]	
What is this? (egg)	1
Where did the egg lie?	2
Find something which is not green	3
How can we tell that it is night time?	4
[Pages 3 & 4]	
Show me the caterpillar	1
Find something that makes us feel warm	2
What will happen next?	3
How will he find food?	4
[Pages 5 & 6]	
Point to the apple	1
What did the caterpillar eat on Monday?	2
How does the caterpillar feel now?	3
Why does the caterpillar want more food?	4

[Saturday page]

What is this? (ice cream and sausage)	1
How are ice cream and sausage different?	2
Find something which is not a fruit	3
What gave the caterpillar tummy ache?	4
If you had a tummy ache what would you do?	4

Level -

APPENDIX 5

SUMMARY

Child A

Child's age in months: 36
Date:16/05/2021

Child A has had lots of 'wow' moments this week. He is now consistently asking when he requires the toilet. He has been independent with hygiene routines and is able to get into and out of his own waterproofs. Child A is a very polite little boy.

Child A's Characteristics of Effective Learning are within Playing and Exploring, particularly seeking challenge. Child A is involved in lots of physical play and constructs tracks using the large blocks followed by jumping across. He will engage in this outside using the large reels and planks. He is encouraged to check for safety and to think about the risk.

Child A will join in with games that other children are playing. On occasion, he has pushed the boundaries with the older children by taking something they are playing with so that they will chase after him, leading to small disputes. However, this is typical 3-year-old behaviour and we have noticed that as he matures, there are less instances of this. Child A is being encouraged to ask if he can join in.

Child A's focus is improving. It will take time and he is only just 3 years old. We read the story 'The Very Hungry Caterpillar' as he was very interested in watching the pre-school caterpillars grow and change into chrysalids. He needed to be refocused by regularly using his name. He counted the fruit pictures accurately pointing to each item up to 4, after which we counted together. Child A started to join in with the refrains and recognised where the story started. You mentioned the alphabet in your focus letter and I would not worry about this yet. We develop the children's focus and listening skills first and then introduce the first phonics sounds. Schools teach phonics first and then blend sounds before using the alphabet.

Child A joined children drawing on large paper on the floor. I have been modelling the tripod pencil grip to him and he was showing me that he could draw big and little triangles. He told me that he likes 'Gruffalo stories' and he was encouraged to draw a picture with the adult suggesting adding extra details such as eyes, nose, etc. He uses both his left and right hand at the moment but can cross his midline.

Child A has been exploring the magnets. We looked at how the trains joined together and he could see the difference between the magnetic attraction/repulsion. We used the trains to look at adding more and taking away. Child A helped build a train track and was able to follow prepositions over and under the bridge.

Child A does throw some toys about, particularly when excited, and we are continuing to model appropriate throwing equipment and games. Child A's need to throw is part of the way he learns, so we are trying to step in early and encourage an appropriate throwing activity in the garden.

You mentioned that Child A becomes frustrated if he cannot do something for himself. This is typical for his age group. We try to help by breaking down the activity into step-by-step parts so it is easier to achieve. We also start off more challenging activities, allowing the child to finish so that they have a positive ending (e.g. starting the zip but letting the child pull up the zipper).

Key person signature: XXXXX Supervisor signature: xxxxx

Date of parent meeting: emailed 17/05/21 Parent signature: xxxxx

Comments from parent/carer:

Thank you – a lovely report and proud to see how he's progressing. Thanks for all you do with him.

Focus for child going forward:

- Increase focus at adult-initiated activity – e.g. story time.
- Support Child A to manage emotions when frustrated.
- Continue to support Child A to follow boundaries within the setting.

Copy of summary emailed to parents: date – 17/05/21

Copy of summary emailed to other setting: (if applicable): date – n/a

INDEX